Praise for *The Big Bang*

"*The Big Bang* is the hippest, the funniest, and the funkiest; lots of frank humor and a sense of cool, heterosexual downtown-ness pervades. Ideal for a young adult or your sister who just got a tiny tattoo that no one can see."   —*O, The Oprah Magazine*

"Artsy, edgy, insatiably hip."   —*San Francisco Chronicle*

"Em & Lo definitely know the ups and downs of sex and dating, but what makes them special in the advice world is their willingness to take it from readers. The result is that everyone gets edified, and hopefully, in the end, satisfied."   —*The Austin Chronicle*

"From the folks at the ultrahip Nerve.com comes a handy sex manual."
                    —*Chicago Sun-Times*

"[A] wry, intelligent take on sex advice . . . hip yet impressively thorough."
                    —*San Francisco Bay Guardian*

"Sexual information, advice, and humor—all presented in Em and Lo's trademark cheeky voices."   —*The Boston Phoenix*

"What you'll love: nonjudgmental suggestions and detailed, illustrated directions that illuminate rather than intimidate."
                    —*The Washington Post*

Em & Lo (Emma Taylor and Lorelei Sharkey), the Emily Posts of the modern bedroom, are the authors of *The Big Bang: Nerve's Guide to the New Sexual Universe.* They write a monthly sex advice column for *Men's Journal* magazine, and have contributed to numerous publications, including *Glamour* and *The Guardian* (UK). After four years as Nerve.com's resident gurus and "astrologists," they can now be found dishing about all things love-, sex-, and star-related on their own website, EmandLo.com. They both live in New York City, where they spend far too much time together.

The Big Bang

NERVE'S GUIDE TO
Sex Etiquette
FOR LADIES and GENTLEMEN

 EM & LO

Emma Taylor and Lorelei Sharkey

Illustrations by Lorelei Sharkey

A PLUME BOOK

PLUME
Published by the Penguin Group
Penguin Group (USA) Inc., 375 Hudson Street, New York, New York 10014, U.S.A.
Penguin Books Ltd, 80 Strand, London WC2R 0RL, England
Penguin Books Australia Ltd, 250 Camberwell Road, Camberwell, Victoria 3124, Australia
Penguin Books Canada Ltd, 10 Alcorn Avenue, Toronto, Ontario, Canada M4V 3B2
Penguin Books India (P) Ltd, 11 Community Centre, Panchsheel Park,
New Delhi—110 017, India
Penguin Books (N.Z.) Ltd, Cnr Rosedale and Airborne Roads, Albany,
Auckland 1310, New Zealand
Penguin Books (South Africa) (Pty) Ltd, 24 Sturdee Avenue, Rosebank,
Johannesburg 2196, South Africa

Penguin Books Ltd, Registered Offices: 80 Strand, London WC2R 0RL, England

First published by Plume, a member of Penguin Group (USA) Inc.

First Printing, February 2004
10   9   8   7   6   5   4   3   2   1

(P) REGISTERED TRADEMARK—MARCA REGISTRADA

LIBRARY OF CONGRESS CATALOGING-IN-PUBLICATION DATA
Taylor, Emma (Emma Jane)
    Nerve's guide to sex etiquette for ladies and gentlemen / Em & Lo—Emma Taylor and Lorelei
Sharkey ; illustrations by Lorelei Sharkey.
      p.   cm.
ISBN 0-452-28509-7 (pbk.)
    1. Sex instruction. 2. Sex customs. 3. Sexual ethics. 4. Dating (Social customs) 5. Mate
selection. I. Title: Sex etiquette for ladies and gentlemen. II. Sharkey, Lorelei III. Nerve.com
(Computer file) IV. Title.
HQ31.T3172 2004
646.7'7—dc22   2003061233

Printed in the United States of America
Set in Tarzana Narrow
Designed by Daniel Lagin

Contents

Dear Reader vii

Acknowledgments ix

CHAPTER I: **Courting** 1

The Art of the Pickup 1

First Dates 16

Going in for the Kiss 29

Second Dates and Beyond 33

CHAPTER II: **Formal Sex** 43

Entertaining 45

The Deed 52

Special Occasions and Situations 62

Virgin Territory 68

CHAPTER III: **Casual Sex** 75

One-Night Stands 78

Booty Calls 82

Group Sex: Threeways, Orgies, and Swinging

with Style 92

CHAPTER IV: **Protocol for Specific Embraces** 109

Oral Operations 109

Geysers, Facials, and Pearl Necklaces 114

Being Anal 118

Sharing Toys 122
Sharing Porn 123
The Fastidious Fetishist 126
Fantasy Island 129
Pristine Potty Talk 136
Virtuous Voyeurism 139
Spanking with Aplomb 142

CHAPTER V: **Love and War** **145**
Long-Term Relationships (LTRs) 145
Intimacy Timeline (chart) 150
Open Relationships 165
The Rules of Disengagement 168
Exes Etiquette 177

CHAPTER VI: **The Unmentionables** **182**
"Impolite" Emissions 182
Safer Sex 194
Performance Anxieties 200
Elements of Style 207

In Conclusion **214**

Dear Reader,

Throughout the history of civilization, etiquette has been subjected to all manner of indignities, not least among them the accusation that it is a bit of a drag. But etiquette is just a fancy word for being considerate of your fellow citizens—whether that means not talking with a mouthful of mushy peas, or showering before receiving a rim job.

It is, in part, a matter of perspective: What is simply good manners to one person is a fastidious rule-for-the-sake-of-a-rule to another. We all have our own measures of character—usually instilled by our parents—even if we refuse to admit to them. Do you cringe at improper grammar and bad spelling in an e-mail? Do you insist on facing forward in an elevator full of strangers? Do you always wipe the seat if you sprinkle when you tinkle? Do you always administer oral sex before requesting it?

Of course, the only perspective that matters here is our own. So the *correct* answers to the above questions are Yes, Yes, Yes, and Yes! There is nothing wrong with being a stickler for politesse, especially when one considers its origin: Good manners are a part of the social contract we voluntarily enter into, in order to create a more harmonious society. And where can we benefit more from a little harmony than in the boudoir?

To be sure, some etiquette is overly stuffy—for example, never serving flavorful Indian or Spanish dishes at a formal dinner. And some etiquette is outmoded, such as a gentleman placing his cloak over a puddle (actually, that one is merely ridiculous). Still, some etiquette is simply sexism in disguise, like men being solely responsible for the condoms. Furthermore, we would be remiss in our duties if we were not to admit that a little Neanderthal behavior is frequently a welcome guest in the bedroom.

There are always exceptions to the rules and times when it is acceptable and appropriate to forgo formal etiquette. For if a gentleman were a gentleman all the time, and a lady a lady through and through, no one would ever have oral sex. But there are some basic rules of engagement that will never go out of style, such as putting the comfort of others before your own (unless, of course, you happen to be dating a masochist).

The remaining rules are constantly evolving to reflect the modes of each generation—the done thing, as it were. We are delighted to take a place in the long tradition of etiquette doyennes—to reaffirm the constants and add some new, saucier suggestions to the canon for these more modern, salacious times. Of course, we expect to blush ferociously when we read whatever sex manners manual will be published fifty years from now. But perhaps then, at least, there will be a sex manners genre to speak of. For it is our immodest goal to make the world a better place, one sex act at a time.

And so, it is with great pleasure that we give you *Nerve's Guide to Sex Etiquette*. If you choose to abide by the enclosed guidelines (for the most part), then you should be rewarded with the most vulgar, uncivilized sex of your life.

Sincerely and affectionately,

Em & Lo, Nerve.com

Acknowledgments

To our families for teaching us our P's and Q's: Allyson, Taylor, Jane, and Bob Sharkey; Sandy Sharkey and Jim Williams; and Becky, Hannah, Muz, and Malcolm Taylor. To Joey Cavella and Jack Wright, our two favorite gentlemen. Dave Jacobs and Gio Dechiara, for asking the tough etiquette questions. The Nerve Gang and Spring Street Networks, for their support, moral and otherwise. The team at Plume: Ryan Harbage, Trena Keating, Brant Janeway, and Katie Walker. Jay Mandel at William Morris. Miss Manners, Emily Post, et al., for teaching us about forks and leaving the dirty bits to us. And finally, Nerve readers the world over, for being the most refined sex animals two advice ladies could hope for.

CHAPTER I
Courting

Dating—pray tell, does anyone do it anymore? It seems as old fashioned as the fedora. In these modern times, people may favor simply hanging out—especially the youngsters. But gentlemen and ladies know that whether this together time is a quick drink at a dive bar, or a five-course meal at Le Cirque followed by an exclusive art opening, it is still simply something to do on a Friday evening with a near stranger with whom you may or may not spend the rest of your life—or at least the rest of your night. Uptown or downtown, traditional or unorthodox, young or old, on a budget or blowing it, dating, hanging, schmoozing, wooing, courting, romancing—whatever you term it, please, dear reader, do it with class.

THE ART OF THE PICKUP

Whence the term "pickup"? Perhaps it stems from that era when the onset of courtship was signaled by a lady dropping her handkerchief and a gentleman retrieving it. Things have gotten rather more complicated since then (though at least we can now all agree that it is vulgar to touch another's snot rag). But we see no reason why "complicated" should mean "humiliating," "soul-destroying," or any of the other adjectives that make a person long for the comforts of the manor. For a start, the modern lady does not wait around to be picked up; she is a proactive seductress, which means that even if the process is humiliating and/or soul-destroying (and yes, sometimes it can be), at least it is a burden shared by the fairer sex.

The most important thing to remember is that every lady and gentleman wants to be wanted. Even if you accidentally pay intimate attention to someone who is betrothed, someone who plays for the other team, or someone who would simply rather be playing bridge, as long as you approach them with good manners and honesty and without invading their personal space, they will be hard-pressed not to be flattered (even if they fail to admit it). A lady or gentleman does not perceive rejection as a shortcoming, and always endeavors not to take it (too) personally—rather, you suffer the interaction gladly because you know it spreads good sexual karma. We promise you, gentle readers, that on your death-bed, asking out Sidney from accounting will not be one of the weighty regrets of your life. So when bent on love, first don a pair of your best underwear, then arm yourself with a liberal supply of interesting small talk, and sally forth unafraid.

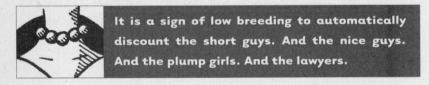

It is a sign of low breeding to automatically discount the short guys. And the nice guys. And the plump girls. And the lawyers.

Pickup Lines

When gentlemen and ladies of a single disposition discuss the art of the pickup, invariably far too much emphasis is placed on the pickup line—as if one, perfectly formed sentence could sweep one's intended off their feet and into a coal-warmed bed. No wonder, then, that so many suitors break out in a cold sweat at the mere thought of composing a pickup line—how can fifteen meager words be expected to do such backbreaking work? Prudence advises you to think of the opening line as simply that: an icebreaker, a conversation starter, an introduction, a how-do-you-do. As a general rule, the only pickup line we officially endorse is "Hi, my name is [your name here]."

However, under the right circumstances, a retro "Care to dance?"

might work—especially at weddings. And though we are far from nostalgic for the preposterous cape-over-the-puddle maneuver, there are other techniques from times past (be they centuries-old or simply junior high) that may be employed in the modern pickup. If you are unfortunate enough to live in a city where smoking in bars is still kosher, keep a Zippo on your person for smooth-lighting moves. Pass a note during a crowded concert or at your local library—you might even include a grade-school-style questionnaire with checkboxes. Or, should you find yourself feeling brave and funny, and should the person in question appear comfortable with witticisms, then take inspiration from all those seven-year-old boys in the school yard who punch the girls they fancy—poke gentle fun at someone's drink order/dance style/pool shot/jukebox pick/calling card/funny-shaped hat. (Note to nincompoops: Do not *actually* punch the lady or gentleman.) You might even host an eighties-themed prom night to provide your social circle an excuse for going retro, from petitioning dates to pinning the corsage to achieving commerce in the back of a white, stretch limo.

Sometimes, situation-specific icebreakers may present themselves, making for more natural segues into a fully fledged pickup. For instance, the sophisticated seducer might try the following openers in these scenarios:

- At the jukebox: "Do they have any Dolly Parton/Rick Astley/Whitesnake/[insert the artist most ridiculously unseemly for your location]?"
- At the launderette: "Do you have change for a dollar?"
- At the buffet table: "May I scoop you some Jell-O?"
- At the library: "Shh!" [said with a cheeky grin as he or she walks past]
- In a long line: "Can you tell I'm kegling right now?"
- At the pool table: "Nice leave!"/"They're playing doubles, care to be my partner?"

⤞ Walking down the street: "Excuse me, I think you dropped this . . ."

⤞ In the cereal aisle at the supermarket: "You should try Kashi, it changed my life. Seriously." (With any luck they will discern your subtext: "Fiber turned me on to anal sex! Seriously.")

⤞ At the gym: "Do you know how this machine works?"

⤞ At the office water cooler: "Hello, I'm [your name], I don't believe we have been introduced. How long have you worked here?"

⤞ At a political rally: "Wanna get high?"

As for the practice of delivering a traditional or crass pickup line with one's tongue firmly in one's cheek, we can only recommend it in good faith for advanced players (*not* playas). It has proven successful far more often in the movies than in real life. But the right lady or gentleman, in the right situation, with the right mischievous twinkle in their eye, in the right light, during the right moon phase, can sometimes execute a hackneyed and pedestrian pickup line *in jest* . . . except, of course, we all know the truth is always spoken in jest. A gentleman or lady may walk past a person and announce, "Was your father a thief? Because he must have stolen the stars to put in your eyes," or, "Nice shoes, wanna fuck?" as long as it is apparent to all parties within earshot that the intent is ironic (and the speaker is not wearing a heavy gold chain or hardhat at the

The Handshake

No element of meeting and greeting suffers the slings and arrows of outrageous misbehavior more so than the handshake. So, please, gather round for this most important lesson: Avoid grips in the extreme—your hand should not pass for a vise or a wet noodle. Instead, your grip should feel firm yet comforting, like a blood-pressure strap after only one—repeat *one*—squeeze of the air ball. Look the person in the eye for the duration of the handshake. Three shakes will suffice. These rules hold fast no matter the gender of the shakers. Women and men work, play, and screw like rabbits as equals, and the proper handshake should reflect this. Gentlemen, the only hand you should be accepting merely the fingers of, rather than the full palm, is your grandmother's.

time). Alternatively, a gentleman or lady may attempt to pick up a frequently hit-on target (such as a bartender) with lines such as "You must get hit on all the time" or "May I hit on you?" This unexpected approach to the whole seduction scene may just tickle their fancy. Or it may warrant a slap in the face. Fair readers, you have been warned.

Buying Drinks

Sending a lady or gentleman a drink is an old standby. However, we must disclaim, this move may be interpreted as cheesy rather than kitschy in certain irony-free zones—perchance Idaho, or Long Island—or by ladies who are frequently sent Slippery Nipples. Thus, we can only recommend this maneuver in good faith to a lady who is buying for a gentleman. If you choose to ignore this suggestion—as you are wont to do—please heed the following hard and fast rules: The well-bred and amiable drink buyer will always offer to purchase an entire round if their intended is among friends. If drinks are delivered to all members of one's party, it would be rude to refuse them (and contrary to all common sense). However, if one is alone, and would rather tweeze one's nose hairs than spend five minutes in conversation with the buyer, then one will graciously decline the cocktail. That said, a gentleman or lady *never* assumes that buying someone a drink means they are owed something (time, conversation, digits). It is gauche, however, to accept a *second* drink as a gift and then refuse to engage in conversation. And after the third free drink, gentlemen and ladies with no romantic interest in the buyer are obliged to make their platonic intentions clear.

To lick one's lips or run one's tongue over one's teeth is not considered an effective method of seduction by anyone with good taste.

Keeping the Conversation Flowing

Oh, felicity! Your opening line (or perhaps simply your generosity of wallet at the bar) garnered a laugh, a smile, a "Delighted to make the pleasure of your acquaintance." Congratulations, now you have to demonstrate a personality! Relax, ladies and gentlemen, breathe, and do not panic. This is where you employ what the experts call "small talk"—and only vulgarians dismiss such chatter as puerile or small-minded. In fact, it is the people who can fluently exchange pleasantries who make our society work. It is churlish to consider oneself above such behavior—if your brain is so full and so busy and you really find it so tiresome to attend to the little civilities, then we strongly urge you to stay home. Gentlemen and ladies ask polite questions, exchange witticisms, pay compliments—all the while avoiding innuendo and controversy. It is imperative to act confident (whether or not you feel that way), but not cocksure: Well-bred ladies and gentlemen are perfectly at home in the middle ground that lies between swaggering aggression and stammering docility. You do not stutter, "I'm not bothering you, am I? Do you need to get back to your friends?" Nor do you pin them in a corner for three hours while regaling them with tales of your athletic/intellectual/comical prowess. Oversharers are unwelcome everywhere, and especially so during a pickup.

 **Gentlemen, reciting quotes from your favorite movie does not constitute appropriate conversation when out on the town.**

The diplomatic lady or gentleman avoids requesting a date or phone number until it is absolutely necessary (i.e., one of you is about to depart). If you are the picker-upper, it is polite to be the quicker picker-upper and take your leave first. When it comes to that time, do not say "How can I reach you" (too presumptuous) or "Give me your number"

(too demanding). A simple "It would be charming to see you again, may I get in touch with you?" will suffice. That way, the object of your affection can decide whether to a) Give you a number, b) Give you an email address, c) Give you the number of the person their ex is currently courting, d) Ask for *your* contact info instead, or e) Look upon you in disgust and then retire. However they respond, you must accept your fate with grace and move on. In the case of "e," this might be a prudent time to remove yourself to the bathroom, especially if you feel tears, a blush, or a foot-stamping tantrum coming on. By the by, if a lady or gentleman proffers an email address or requests *your* info, this should not necessarily be interpreted as a rejection—some people (especially the frequently stalked) simply prefer it that way.

The most refined matchmakers keep their intentions to themselves, arrange the "coincidental" meeting of two incredibly compatible acquaintances, and allow Fate to handle the rest. Anything more conspicuous—for instance, "X meet Y; X bakes the best pot brownies and Y is hung like a horse"— is gauche.

The Ten Commandments of the Pickup

A person who is what they seem and pretends to be nothing more will excel in the art of seduction. A genuine, sincere gentleman or lady will be welcomed into most conversations, provided that he or she is a person of some natural ability, wit, or charm. The more out-of-character one's approach, the more awkward the whole encounter is destined to be, and the more awkward your intended is going to feel. Plus, to live a lie now means trouble is bound to come later. That said, there are certain things that should *never* be said or done during a pickup, no matter how "naturally" they may come to you:

1. A gentleman or lady does not attempt a pickup at a doctor's office (at a dentist's office is occasionally acceptable), at a funeral, or in front of someone's parents. A gentleman or lady never attempts to pick up their doctor, dentist, dental assistant, aerobics instructor, professor (at least while class is in session), boss, assistant, or intimate waxer. And a gentleman or lady never attempts to pick up their patient, client, or underling.

2. A gentleman does not wordlessly dry-hump a stranger from behind on the dance floor (the same goes for the ladies).

3. If a pickup line turns into a conversation, gentlemen and ladies are earnestly advised not to limit their conversation to remarks on the weather and the heat of the room—this shows a poverty of ideas that is truly pitiable. In addition, it is considered gauche to discuss any of the following: astrology, college majors, exes, reproductive rights legislation, infidelity, or children. Safe topics include: the bar (et cetera) that you are in, if he or she lives in the neighborhood, what he or she does for a living, some inane law your mayor recently passed, his or her darts skills, HBO, mullet websites, and whether or not Tivo has revolutionized their life.

4. A gentleman or lady never requests contact information merely to be the one who scores the most digits; the pickup is not a numbers game. However, it is perfectly acceptable to build confidence by talking to strangers wherever you go, even if you have no interest in bedding them—as long as you take care not to mislead them as to your intentions. Flirting is exceedingly prone to misinterpretation; take pains not to evince a false or inappropriate impression. In fact, true ladies and gentlemen flirt in the middle ground between careless abandon and obsessive discretion.

5. At one time it was considered gauche for a lady to refuse the attentions of one gentleman and then accept those of another in

the same evening—or worse, to accept the attentions of two men in the same evening. The romantically inclined now understand that ladies and gentlemen of a single disposition may receive attention willy-nilly—whether that attention comes in the form of drinks bought, numbers exchanged, or vague promises hinted at. However, once saliva has been exchanged, it is considered polite to be a little more focused in one's attentions.

6. A gentleman or lady never lies during a pickup (about their occupation, position, intentions, et cetera). The end (getting a number) does not justify the means (being a fraud).

7. A gentleman or lady never compliments someone on a body part. *Sincere* compliments will be appreciated if they focus on something more specific and unexpected, like an item of clothing, a certain way with the pool cue, a particular selection in the grocery store, et cetera.

8. A gentleman or lady never looks someone in the boobs or genitals while talking, even if that person's daring neckline or visible pantaloons line (VPL) has a paralyzing effect on their thought process. All citizens—no matter how tastelessly or recklessly they are dressed—deserve your utmost respect. *Eye contact,* readers—it is the ultimate compliment.

9. A gentleman never assumes when a lady crosses her legs on the subway and accidentally exposes her briefs, or leans forward at the bar and shows a bra strap or a little more cleavage, that it is an intentional come-on to said gentleman. It is the height of vulgarity to stare at this item of clothing as if you suspected they had stolen it from you, or wore something that was not their own. The majority of women are oblivious to their fleeting Sharon Stone impersonations on a crowded subway before a hectic day at work, or at a crowded bar after a hectic day at work. A true lady is annoyed by strange men looking under her hemline or down her blouse. And we suspect that cads would not be privy to so many hypnotic white triangles if they did not spend so much time staring at women's crotches and chests.

10. A gentleman or lady does not invade another's personal space via excessive hand-on-elbow, hand-on-knee, hand-on-the-small-of the-back, close talking, et cetera, unless he or she has conclusive evidence it is welcome. Each gentleman and lady has a particular threshold for the touchy-feely: What one considers salacious behavior, another considers just being amiable. When in doubt, the gentleman or lady always errs on the side of caution.

Should you disregard any of the above ten commandments, you must expect and accept swift punishment, whether in the form of a slap to the face, a knee to the groin, or a life of solitude and onanism. Should you, on the other hand, find yourself in the presence of such a sinner, it is beneath you as a lady or gentleman to dignify their ignorance with an outburst of verbal or physical abuse, no matter how much it is deserved. Instead, simply walk away and allow karma to punish the jackholes of the world. In the most extreme situations, insulting them in a deferential manner ("Why good sir, I do believe I have some paint to watch dry, if you would excuse me") is the most you may do; this will not administer the complete etiquette lesson they so desperately need, but it may keep your head from exploding in fury.

Picking Up Interference

A gentleman or lady is never an enabler; infidelity is to be neither encouraged nor rewarded. To discover the marrieds who walk among us, it is a simple matter of remembering: ring finger, next to the pinkie, on the *left* hand. If you find yourself in a hotel bar in the vicinity of a sales conference of some kind, then you should be wary of a band of slightly indented, untanned skin on said finger of those you would hit upon. And to those of you philistines who remove your wedding band for a night on the town: Shame on you. Now turn around while we administer your spanking. Besides, there are abundant philistines who get off on pursuing the marrieds, rings aplenty. And to those of you philistines who pursue the marrieds: Shame on you. Marriage is not a thing to be put to the test merely to ascertain whether it can withstand your charms—that would be like dropping a kitten off a skyscraper to verify the rumors about cats' uncanny landing skills. No matter if it is not your kitten—it is nonetheless a cute, fluffy little thing that should be treated with kindness.

In the absence of a ring, sadly, there is no secret handshake or funny little dance to let a lady or gentleman know whether someone is on or off the market (and those traffic-light parties at which the available wear green and the taken wear don't-go-there red went out with girdles). But does it really matter? Let us take a wild guess and say there is a one in two chance that this charming young thing is happily cohabited. But there is, perhaps, a

Dating a Friend's Relative

Pursuing a member of a friend's nuclear family is a thing never to be done casually (long-lost third cousins are, however, fair game). At times, however, Cupid strikes us unaware and without our assent; suddenly our best friend's sibling, whom we have teased since grade school, is all grown up and—pardon our French—smokin' hot. Such salacity, once aroused, allows little room for reason or conscience. In the case of a very close friend and a very close relative, it is advisable to wait out the crush a month or two to ascertain its  stamina. If it appears to have staying power, then you must state your intentions to your friend—do not request their permission if you are unwilling to take "no" for an answer—and then begin the wooing. And here, ladies and gentlemen, we learn the importance of *always* acting with manners, of making etiquette an integral part of one's character rather than just a show for the fairer sex (whichever sex you consider fairer). Your best friend is familiar with your *true* character, all your foibles and maybe even some of your fetishes. If your true self is loutish and vulgar, you may have to sacrifice a friendship for true love; if, on the other hand, you are a proper gentleman or lady down to the bone, you are infinitely more likely to be welcomed into that friend's family.

one in a *hundred* chance that your respective pheromones will waltz gracefully across the dance floor together, making the two of you laugh inanely, exclaim "I love this band!" to a song you have never heard, and then monopolize each other's dance cards. It is not necessary to distract yourself from the pickup in progress by trying to figure out whether a person is available—it is their job to tell you that, assuming that a) They are not one of those aforementioned philistines, and b) Your attempted pickup could not be easily mistaken for a market research interview/request for a donation to Greenpeace.

Additionally, the sensitive gentleman or lady will understandably want to lower his or her chances of accidentally asking out someone who plays for the other team. Unfortunately for straight people with no gaydar or gay people with no straight-alert, there is no sexual-orientation ring finger. Gay/straight checklists exist only on prime-time sitcoms. And only a vulgarian would give someone a lunchtime poll in the middle of a bar: "Check this out, you win five million dollars from the Publishers Sweepstakes and the same day that Big Ed gives you the check, aliens land on earth and say they're going to blow up the world in two days. Are you gay?" Lovers would do well to approach the situation as the cast of Saturday Night Live approached the painfully androgynous Pat. As with the ambiguously single, one should treat the ambiguously gay/straight like any other pickup; and if, perchance, your smooth moves are more obvious than their sexual preference, they will inform you that you are barking up the queer tree. It is the correct thing to remember that getting rejected because you are on the other team is infinitely more pleasing than getting rejected because, though you are on the right team, you are simply not sufficiently alluring.

Those who suspect they are on the receiving end of a pickup and are, shall we say, otherwise engaged, should walk a steady line between premature presumptuousness and the disingenuous omission of pertinent facts. Sadly, there is no secret formula for deciphering the code of someone's particular brand of flirtation, so the best course of action to take when you are romantically infringed upon is to drop mention of your significant other as casually and nonchalantly as if you were speaking of the weather. If you are in a committed, monogamous relationship, but are "allowed" the freedom of innocent flirting, you must stop *long* of giving someone the impression that you are available for an afternoon of hardcore butt pirating at their earliest convenience.

The Art of Rejection: Strangers

Attention never fails to be flattering, but it frequently fails to arouse salacity, whether due to protruding nose hair, pleated pants, wrong gender, et cetera. While it is not fair to lead someone on by giving them a fake number (bad, *bad* etiquette) or one of those commercial rejection lines (worse, *worse* etiquette), there is such a thing as killing them softly. You will make this world a better place if you act kindly. Try, "You flatter me, but I am seeing someone right now." We are not suggesting you lie, of course . . . but a small *exaggeration* is perfectly in order. Perhaps you are taking a somewhat permanent break from dating men who resemble Janet Reno or women who have the charisma of a shoehorn, in which case a simple "I'm taking a break from dating" will suffice. It is not entirely untrue: You are taking a mini-break from dating until this excruciating pickup attempt is over. Of course, a simple, polite, "I'm flattered but not interested, thanks" is admirably honest. But readers, none of us is running for political office here, so there is no need to go frightening the horses. One of etiquette's many pet causes is cushioning easily bruised egos.

A note to the hetero gentlemen: You are less frequently the recipient of a come-on, and thus you are less practiced at rejecting an unwelcome one. Which means you are frequently awkward and weird about it. Gentlemen should pay special attention to the etiquette of rejection because it is of utmost importance that ladies not be discouraged in their seductions. Do not acquiesce just to avoid hurting her feelings, but do not treat her like a desperate Donna either. She is not desperate for hitting on you (who absconded with *your* self-esteem, anyway?), she just knows what she wants and goes after it when she wants it. And ladies, do not take it personally if you receive an impolite rejection from a gentleman; he has simply had less practice in the art of rejection than you.

A note to the hetero ladies: You are less frequently the active pursuer and thus you are less familiar with the sting of rejection. (Which is why every lady should attempt at least one pickup to experience it firsthand, in the same way that all first-class citizens should wait tables at least once in order to empathize with servers the world over.) Approaching a person in a bar requires a degree of bravery greater than that summoned to undergo root-canal treatment or listen to a Celine Dion album in its entirety. So please, readers, be gentle souls. And dear sirs, do not take it personally if you suffer an impolite rejection from a lady; she has heard a lot of vulgar catcalls and objectionable pickup lines in her life and is used to putting up walls.

On a final note, if your ardent admirer breaches every pickup etiquette rule in the book (*this* book, natch), you should feel free to kick them to the curb like the dirty dog they are.

The Art of Rejection: Friends

Letting a friend down gently is an onerous task, especially if they weigh more than you. *Ba dum ching!* But seriously, ladies and gentlemen, very rarely do strangers approach you on the subway, compliment your khakis, and then beseech you for a date (despite what the breath-mint commercials would have you believe). If this were to happen, you could simply say, "Thank you, but I'm not interested," if you were not interested, and that would be that. Or if you are a card-carrying member of the EPA (Ego

Protection Agency), you would use one of the exaggerations we proposed in "The Art of Rejection." But it is infinitely more likely that you will be propositioned by someone you know—an acquaintance, a coworker, even a good friend—and not be interested.

First and foremost, it is artless and inconsiderate to accept an invitation for a first date or anything remotely resembling a date if you are convinced deep down that monkeys would migrate from your posterior before you would ever go to first base with the person in question. If someone has not explicitly conveyed their intentions, but you swear you can feel them undressing you with their eyes, then it is polite to start by dropping hints—big, dense, two-ton hints—about other people you are interested in, about things going on with your significant other (real or imagined), about how refreshing it is to have a platonic friend to parley with about this stuff, et cetera. This *should* work. In a rational world where hormones were not clouding our logic and good sense, this *would* work. But damn it, readers, we do not live in that kind of world! Your admirer may misconstrue the conversations about your romantic life as sure signs of your romantic interest in *them*. They might be so taken with you as to interpret the way you stir your coffee as hard evidence of your undying love and lust for them. (Hope is a thing with feathers and no brain.)

If you suspect that your storytelling has failed to put them off, or worse, they attempt to court you, then it is time, ladies and gentlemen for The Talk. A well-bred lady or gentlemen memorizes phrases for trying times such as these: "I really care about you as a *friend*," "I really value our friendship and don't want to jeopardize it," "Thank you, but I'm not interested . . ." [Insert platitude here.] Prudence advises that if you fear you are leading a person on, then in their eyes you probably are. A gentleman or lady lays down the law. A gentleman or lady is a rock, is an island.

FIRST DATES

So your poise, your composure, your sangfroid, your *je ne sais quois* have procured a number—but now what is a person to do? If only going to Disney World were a viable option. Chances are you are not in the vicinity of Dollywood, either, so the burden is upon you to put forward something sophisticated. You would do well to remember that this is only a first date, so it is prudent to keep things simple—a gentleman or lady does not blow their wad prematurely. Nor do they desire to make the first date a "challenge" in order to ascertain their companion's skill on the court/reaction to a work of art/figure in a bathing suit. (We insist that you save that for the third or fourth date, see Second Dates and Beyond.) In addition, the date should not involve some activity that precludes conversation (for example, the opera). But no person desires to spend an entire evening in an empty room with nothing but conversation to fill the space—far from a date, that is a police interrogation. Rather, a gentleman or lady settles for activities that offer a mild distraction and some potential to spark conversation. For instance, a mosh pit hardly screams "romance," but a mellifluous concert in a small, local bar is above tolerable. (You would be sensible to eschew folk music—that could quell even Hugh Hefner's sex drive.) A gentleman or lady may escort their date to an area of their town/city that they are particularly fond of and somewhat savvy about, for instance, dim sum in Chinatown followed by bubble tea at a little tea shop around the corner. When making plans together, do not be fascist about your suggestions, but do not be wishy-washy either: "I don't care, whatever you want" is never a good answer to any question. A gentleman or lady always forms an opinion.

A gentleman or lady always turns off his or her cell phone and avoids looking at watches during a date.

Prepping

When prepping for a date, a gentleman or lady takes a casual-yet-thoughtful approach. It is not recommended to show up in a suit, lest you give the appearance of being anal. However, looking as if you put a modicum of effort into your appearance is endearing. Do not try to impersonate another, however. For instance, if you never wear makeup, it would be foolish to allow your Avon Lady friend to give you a Ricki Lake makeover before the date. Gentlemen, tanktops are for ladies and Calvin Klein models only. And *trim your nose hair*. That goes for the ladies, too. One dangling, stray strand is like Niagara Falls on the hot flames of your date's libido. And men, do not just wash your balls: The well-bred gentleman takes a full shower. Finally, if you are under the weather, do not go. It is not considered being a "trooper"; nobody wants your germs. But when you call to cancel, it is elegant to reschedule with specifics during the same conversation so your friend is satisfied you are speaking the truth.

The Grand Entrance

Only the savage fails to be on time for a date. Sticklers for punctuality like to say, "If I am not on time, assume I am dead." Make that your mantra, gentle readers, because when it comes to first dates, there is no such thing as fashionably late. If your date is late and has not called with an extremely good excuse after twenty minutes, it is not ungracious to depart in order to seduce another lady or gentleman at a neighboring bar.

Upon espying your date, it is elegant to greet them with gusto—no limp handshakes (see sidebar on p. 4). A dry kiss on the cheek is agreeable, and a hug would not be out of place if you had a particularly intense pickup, or the first date is coming *after* you have already had sex. If you are not European, always limit the cheek kiss to *one* cheek; two is awkward, not to mention pretentious. And remember to make eye contact from here on out (though the educated citizen knows the difference between eye contact and creepy staring contests).

Small to Medium-Size Talk

Conversation is an art form. A gentleman or lady always asks questions . . . and actually listens to the answers. Nothing is so offensively ill-bred as gazing absentmindedly at some hottie shooting pool in the back of the bar while your date tells you how they ate their lunch in the bathroom during high school. It is the height of vulgarity to be anything other than exclusively devoted to your companion for the evening. This behavior is an explicit declaration, on your part, that the most trifling object deserves your attention, more than all that might be uttered by the lovely in front of you. And as for the boors who allow themselves to keep up, by the telegraph of eye and face, a communication with others during a date, you deserve no one's attention, not even ours. Good day, sir!

A gentleman or lady never asks questions simply to provide their own answers. And you would do well to remember that there *is* such a thing as a stupid question. It is not correct to ask, "Where do you see yourself in five years?" "Tell me all your thoughts on God . . ." "You're pro-life, right?" "If you could be any kind of tree/animal/Burger King entrée, what kind would you be?" "Are those real?" "What kind of car do you drive?" or any other subtle questions aimed at determining your date's net worth. And it is gauche to talk about your ex on a first date; nothing good can come of it . . . *ever*. If your ex was the greatest thing since sliced bread, you will make your date feel inferior; if your ex was crazier than Norman Bates, you will make your date feel superior to the point of questioning why they are socializing with the likes of you. As with the pickup, safe topics of first-date conversation include your date's job, past travels, where they grew up, how they grew up, recent movies/books/TV, and the role of irony in T-shirt slogans. Compliment, compliment, compliment (but no more than three times in a night). And gentle readers, do not make shit up. If you are on the receiving end of a compliment, always take it gracefully.

Attitude Adjustment

Confidence—as opposed to swollen-headed cockiness—is always sexy. If you are cursed with the first-date jitters, do whatever it takes to calm your nerves, whether that is yoga, lucky underwear, or a pre-date shot with a good friend who will blow smoke up your posterior. If you do not feel confident, then it is prudent to *fake it*. With that in mind, it is wise not to take yourself (or your date) too seriously—after all, it is no more than a first date with the possible future mother/father of your children. (Ay, there's the rub!) The same goes for nervous giggles. Ladies, you may have once been told that it is cute and endearing, but forty-five minutes of high-pitched squeaks can really start to grate on a gentleman's nerves.

There is, in addition, a difference between sexual confidence and sexual braggadocio. It is absolutely refined to be sexy, to know what you want, and to pursue it. However, prattling on over dinner about what great head you give just to be provocative, is Tacky with a capital "T." Ladies and gentlemen walk the walk *when they get there*, and save the talk.

 Ladies, do not read women's magazines for dating advice—unless you are in the market for a *Maxim* reader and/or a boor. Gentlemen, do not read men's magazine for dating advice—unless *you* are a boor.

Money Talks

Dates may be cheap, but they ain't never free. So who coughs up? Whoever did the asking pays for the date, be they a gentleman or a gentle lady. This is the twenty-first century, dear readers, and thus it is provincial and outmoded to assume the man always gets it. However, those who have been asked out, whether male or female, should always assume they will be going dutch to avoid disappointment and come prepared with cash to avoid washing dishes. When the check comes, offer to go halvsies. If you do end up sharing the bill, then the person who ordered the more expensive items on the menu should offer to pay their full share, while the person whose items constitute less than half the total must still offer to pitch in exactly half of the check; use the leftover cash for a carriage ride in the park or joint admission to a strip club. Alternately, if a date resists an offer to go dutch and would like to pay your way, you may insist firmly but gently that you pitch in, if you are so inclined. However, if this initiates a battle of the Amexes, then you must defer to the person who did the asking out (perchance it is the miles). The refined citizen may turn this into an opportunity to suggest an extension of the date—or even a second date—by offering, "Let me get the next one," or "Cocktails around the corner are on me." And though we would like to believe that everyone knows better by now, we should just point out that no matter how much your date spends on dinner or how many compliments they give you, you do not owe them a thing in the booty department—not even a kiss.

Blind Dates

The blind date is alive and well, thanks to Personals and well-intentioned grandmothers. Still, the mere thought of a setup can cower the bravest souls, for Murphy's Law all but guarantees that your blind date will be a loud talker with halitosis and a goiter. So why do otherwise intelligent beings ever agree to them? Call it hope triumphing over experience. Or perhaps just living on the edge. We lull ourselves into believing that this date could be "The One." In the process, we end up unintentionally imbuing our date with a hundred mystical qualities before we have even met them, so that when we finally do meet, we are sure to be disappointed. The biggest faux pas is taking this disappointment personally—and then taking it out on the date. After all, they are a complete stranger, we owe them nothing. *Au contraire!* Heed this, ladies and gentlemen: By agreeing to a date, indeed just by being a part of this society, you are bound by the social contract to act with courtesy and kindness, regardless of the growth the size of a football protruding from your date's neck.

There are several ways to ease the inevitable pain of the blind date. First, plan it with care. No dinner (too long), no movies (too antisocial), no weekend getaways to Niagara Falls (too freaking weird). We insist that you settle for one coffee, one drink, or one quick bite on your lunch break—the operative word here being *one*. It is infinitely more pleasant to extend a date on the fly than it is to cut one short. If either of you is a fan of pool or darts, then you are in luck, dear friends: Both activities allow for conversation while providing a mild distraction if that conversation should prove to be less than scintillating. Set up your escape route beforehand: Have somewhere to be later. It makes a bad date more bearable if you have something pleasant to look forward to. And it is polite to let your date know upfront that you will eventually have to dash, so they do not feel injured when you do so. If it is going well, you can be old-fashioned and save something for the second date—a true gentleman or lady knows that delayed gratification always makes things hotter.

Once the blind date has begun, it is proper to let it play out. We think forty-five minutes minimum is a nice gesture. Ladies and gentlemen, you have struck a deal with Cupid: You give up forty-five minutes of your life for the chance to meet the love of your life (or at least get the best head of your life). If this fails to transpire, well, then, how unfortunate it is to be you. But as a well-mannered dater, you must nevertheless make good on your end of the deal. Call it karma. And no, staying until you finish your drink is not leading someone on, it is simply elegant behavior. As is being attentive and pleasant for that three-quarters of an hour. We do not care if you realize within the first thirty seconds you have no desire to know or do this person. Rudeness is not an appropriate way to let them know you are not interested. This is a human being before you; do not dare to crush them like a bug. At the very least, turn the encounter into a learning experience—they must know something you do not. Just because a human interaction is an isolated occurrence does not make it meaningless or worthless.

Thusly: It is not correct to excuse yourself to the bathroom and never come back. It is not correct to fake anything: a cramp, a food-allergy reaction, an epileptic attack, a bad case of the runs, et cetera. It is not correct to have a friend call you with an emergency—this trick has been done to death. And it is certainly not correct to have any friends stop by to save you.

There are only two exceptions to the forty-five minute rule: when your date is a liar or a complete vulgarian. Some citizens feel the ends justify the means, that it does not matter how you get to the date, even if it be under false pretenses, so long as you get there. These Neanderthals post decades-old photos or purloined images of their good-looking cousins in their online personal ads. Now, gentle readers, we are not speaking of a couple of extra pounds or a change in sideburn length. We speak rather of a hundred pounds or the sudden loss of a full head of hair (not by choice). Or maybe they exaggerated their stature by more than, oh, say, a *foot*. In addition, the following fall into the "complete vulgarian" category: physical aggression, racism, homophobia, sexism, Polish jokes, or any of those imbecilic lines like "Nice outfit, it'd look even better in a pile on my bedroom floor" unless uttered in jest (see Pickup Lines earlier—however, if *you* fail to find it amusing, then it is not). Actually, there is one more exception to the forty-five minute rule: If your date shows up in a cape. In any of these cases, it is perfectly correct to say you feel you have been mislead or are uncomfortable, and then depart.

It looks gauche in the extreme to schedule more than one date during a night. The only exceptions are blind dates (which includes first Personals dates).

When Someone Else Is Dating Your Intended

What happens when you have found that perfect someone, the person you suspect could be the illustrious "One," and they are inconveniently dating another? You may be honest, but you must wear your honesty with reservation. Confess your feelings, but refrain from putting any undue pressure on the object of your obsession. For example, it would be beneath you to say, "If I can't have you, no one will [maniacal laugh]," or perhaps, "I'm going to eat my goldfish if you don't go out with me." Once you have lobbed the ball into their court, grant them the time and space to decide whether to return the serve—or hit the net. You must allow them to make the decision alone. If you encourage them in any way to leave, lie to, or cheat on their current lover, you are nothing more than a desperate, pathetic heathen who deserves to roam the deserted streets of Solitude for the rest of your days. If your true love eventually takes pity on you and decides to give you a second glance, it is necessary that you give them a little more than twenty-four hours to acclimate to life without their recently axed ex. But that is far too much waiting, you protest! We recommend taking the time to teach yourself chess. If they indeed are The One, they will be worth the wait. And if not, a well-honed chess game is a becoming social accessory for any lady or gentleman. One final word to the wise: In some cases, what is keeping two people apart is what draws them together. The obstacle allows you to fantasize how perfect the union would be, if only the obstacle were not there—like Romeo and Juliet (sans the double suicide). Once that obstacle is removed, the reality may turn out to be rather, for lack of a more delicate term, *blah*. Ladies and gentlemen, be careful what you wish for.

Table Manners

Should you find yourself partaking of any culinary delights during a date, the following twenty simple rules will help you digest with grace. Remember, one should be an animal in the bedroom, not the dining room.

1. Never sit next to each other on one side of a table unless you are being filmed for a reality TV show. It is unsettling to the other restaurant guests, who are made to feel like players on a stage with you two as the audience. The PDA you are invariably tempted to engage in because you have decided to sit side-by-side may also make your fellow diners uncomfortable and unable to digest their food properly. Be adults and sit facing each other. The romance of staring into each other's eyes over a candle-lit table should be enough for any thoughtful lady and gentleman.

2. When you sit down, gentle digester, put your napkin in your lap immediately.

3. Gentlemen, do not presume to order for the lady. She is an adult: She can make up her own mind and she can speak for herself.

4. Do not order "just a salad." To do so suggests you would rather honor an unhealthy obsession with empty calories than wholeheartedly embrace the date and all its attendant pleasures, including the gastronomic ones. Inversely, do not order the lobster, unless it has been unequivocally established that you are indeed paying.

5. No cell phones at the table, please, even if you are dining at Denny's. (Good manners do not discriminate against even the

tackiest of eating establishments.) If you absolutely, positively *must* attend to a call, keep your phone on vibrate, but for heaven's sake do not whip it out. Wait for an appropriate pause in the conversation to excuse yourself from the table to retrieve or make that call. However, we cannot impress upon you enough: It better be an emergency.

6. If you have to use the powder room, all you have to say is "Excuse me please" or "Will you excuse me for just a moment?" Your date does not need to be told that you are off to evacuate your bowels.

7. You must always wash your hands after using the restroom, even if you are a coordinated, hands-free pisser. Only *you* can prevent the spread of Hepatitis A.

8. Ladies and gentlemen do not begin eating until their date has also been served. Do not even disturb your silverware until their dish, delivered by the server, has made contact with the table linen. Only in the case of the kitchen royally flubbing up and your date insisting that you begin, may you do so; however, even then it is advised that you have the server return your dish to the kitchen to be kept warm or reprepared to coincide with the progress of your date's dinner.

9. Your date knows what you are eating, for they can see it on your plate. They do not need to see it in your mouth. (This extends to even the most informal occasions, including movie screenings—noisy popcorn munching can be like daggers to your neighbors' ears.)

10. Even if your modern relationship has rapidly progressed to the open burping policy stage (see p. 149), that is no excuse for doing so in public. If it can not be avoided, nonchalantly bring your napkin to your lips to muffle the closed-mouth emission. And as a true lady or gentleman, you should automatically know to excuse yourself to the bathroom when you realize the bean dip was

a mistake. The occasional "pull my finger" joke among really, *really* close friends is acceptable, but never at the dinner table. And never with someone you are hoping to poke with that finger later.

11. *Chew.* Take your sweet time, for eating is a pleasure, not a race. Finish one mouthful before you take another. (This will additionally help with the "no farting in public" rule, since inadvertently ingesting surplus air is the main culprit of gas attacks.)

12. Ladies and gentlemen should be particularly careful how they manage so ticklish a delicacy as corn on the cob, frankfurters, bananas, lollipops, ice-cream cones, and oysters, lest the exhibition encourage undesirable or at least untimely advances.

13. Engage in appropriate dinner conversation. Discussing the etymology of "The Dirty Sanchez" is unacceptable—save that for when you retire to the bar.

14. Never reach across someone at the table: Always ask, "Would you please pass the [blank]?"

15. Even if you ask the waiter nicely, you may *never* finish off the half-eaten piece of tiramisu or the half-drunk glass of barbera left behind by someone at the next table over. In fact, do not even presume to nibble on food from your date's plate unless they offer first.

16. If it is apparent your date is suffering from entrée envy, you may offer to trade plates. This is not required, of course, though a happily fed lady or gentleman is usually far more amenable to a good night kiss, a second date, or late night nookie.

17. It is offending to good taste as well as common sense to gesture with your silverware. You do not need to create a more colorful picture by using a cherry tomato on a fork as if it were a pointer— one wrong move, and said tomato could go flying across the restaurant into someone's décolletage.

18. Similarly, do not use your fingers or silverware to dislodge food

from between your teeth. Suffer in silence until you can retreat to the restroom to deal with the offending tidbit.

19. Be courteous to the waitstaff. Never snap, clap, cry "Waiter!" or worse, "Garçon!" to get your attendant's attention; wait until you catch your server's eye, then simply nod, gently raise your eyebrows, or, as a last resort, raise your hand. If you are in any way rude and obnoxious to the service-industry professionals, it will only suggest to your date that you have the potential to be rude and obnoxious to anyone.

20. If you are picking up the bill, then do tip 20 percent lest you look like a cheap bastard.

Saying Good Night

Saying good night may mean "Good-bye." Of course, if the date is going swimmingly, it may well mean "How do you like your eggs?" However, one should never *assume* one is going to score. Similarly, one should never pressure someone to accompany one home. If it is meant to be, it will happen naturally, without coercion. And begging is neither polite nor sexy (unless you are already naked and willingly playing "master and servant"). Even if both parties are eager to get their freak on, it is not rude to delay gratification and wait for the second, third, or even tenth date (for more on closing the deal, see p. 44).

But what if you reach the bottom of your grande iced-decaf soy mocha and you know, in your heart of hearts, you would rather suffer the indecencies of attending a taping of *The Jerry Springer Show* than go on a second date? A simple "It was nice seeing you" is all that is required. Resist your natural instinct to make promises you cannot or will not keep. If you must, simply add an "I'll email you" to wrap things up nicely. Of course, that will mean you are *required* to follow through. Take solace in the fact that it is infinitely easier to let someone down gently via email. If, in a moment of weakness, you accidentally blurt out "I'll call you,"

then you must call. Any thoroughbred citizen versed in the lessons of
karma would.

When you make that call or send
that email—whether after one or
even several dates—you do not necessarily have to tell the whole truth
(for sometimes the truth hurts, and
sometimes they cannot handle the
truth). It is not just Blanche in *A
Streetcar Named Desire* who depends on the kindness of strangers.
So here is your chance to be kind.

> ### The Long Walk Home
>
> It is polite to offer to
> see someone home,
> whether that means put-
> ting them in a cab or
> walking them to their
> door. However, if your
> date refuses your offer more than twice,
> you must graciously accept the fact that
> they would prefer to go gently into that
> good night *alone*. Resist, with every fiber
> of your being, all temptations to pout or
> take it personally.

Be specific about the qualities you admire in them (their exquisite taste
in domestic beer, for example), and be very general about those that
make a relationship impossible (avoid mentioning that you could never
be seen in public with someone who wears Docksiders). Blame it on the
pheromones, an unfortunate "lack of chemistry." It is the truth, but it is
also generic enough not to sting too strongly—being dumped is never
quite as painful or regrettable when one can chalk it up to evolutionary
psychology. "Great hanging out with you, but I just didn't feel like we
clicked. Good luck with [whatever project of theirs you discussed]. All
the best . . ." You are not obliged to explain it any further than that, and
you do not have to stay in touch. If they are sensitive creatures, they will
appreciate the closure and the gesture (even if they can see right
through your cheap lies). In addition, this will deliver you from the
trauma of trying to hide from them for the rest of your days.

If they preempt your closer with a request for a second date, put off
any concrete planning with a simple "Let's talk tomorrow." This has the
benefit of casting you in a favorable light, for you will not appear to be
making any snap decisions or rushing to judgment. However, if you hap-

pen to be the proud owner of balls or labes of steel, you may *delicately* lay the no-chemistry line on them right then and there.

GOING IN FOR THE KISS

Most unfortunately, there are coxcombs among us who refer to making a move as "going in for the kill." However, leaning in for that first kiss should not be considered some kind of predatory attack, a forceful champing at the bit with excessive salivation. Instead, it should be thought of as an intimate moment *shared* between two people that can run the gamut from sweet and romantic to hot and heavy. Unfortunately, too many people mistake "hot and heavy" for "wet and messy." These people are the bad kissers among us. Do not hate them, for they know not what they do (usually because no one has the heart or presence of mind to set them straight). Hence, *everyone* believes they alone have turned lip-locking into an art form. But *someone* has got to be inspiring the countless tales told round water coolers about the "spin cyclist." Who knows, perhaps it is you, dear reader. Follow the rules below to make certain it is not.

- Ladies and gentlemen, do not lick your lips as you go in for the kiss. This is the equivalent of a renowned opera singer hacking up a loogie on stage in order to clear his throat before an aria.
- Your mouth is not a jack-in-the-box. Ergo, every time you open it, your tongue should *not* automatically pop out. Work up to this most precocious of French maneuvers. When in doubt, follow this order of operations during any given kissing session: 1) Closed mouth, 2) Opened mouth, no tongue, 3) Opened mouth, just the hint of tongue, 4) Full-on tongue probing. Whether that four-step process takes a half hour or thirty seconds to complete, the

buildup is infinitely preferable to sticking out one's tongue and saying "Ahhh" as one's patented opening move.

-- Do not open your mouth so much wider than your partner's that it appears as if you are trying to eat their head. Kissing is not a Mick Jagger impersonation contest.

-- Tongue-flicking your partner's uvula as if it were a boxing bag must never be attempted by anyone wishing to float high above the depths of vulgarity, not to mention stupidity.

-- Do *not* make a beeline for the boobs, the ass, or the crotch the instant the lips have locked, especially during a first kiss or during kisses early on in the dating process. It is one thing if you are both living out the elevator scene from *Fatal Attraction*. It is quite another if you are strolling along the promenade under the moonlit sky, having done nothing but hand-holding up until this point. In most cases, romance should take priority over unadulterated lasciviousness; you will both wish to savor the moment, so focus on the kissing. Do not denigrate it or distract yourselves from its beauty by rushing to the naughty bits. True ladies and gentlemen, for the most part, take their sweet time.

-- Only the most hopeless of souls employs the sucker punch. Sneaking up on someone (especially someone you have never kissed before) and planting one on them by surprise so they cannot act quickly enough *not* to kiss you is the epitome of rudeness, to say nothing of desperation. You may, however, grab your date by the hand, push them up against a wall and plant one on them passionately, *so long as* there is not even the slightest hint of hesitation in their constitution. That three-step process should give you enough time to accurately assess your date's response and abort the kiss if need be.

-- Likewise, grabbing someone's face is romantic so long as you are not holding their head to keep them from pulling away. Putting

someone in a headlock so they cannot escape your kisser is not
only rude, it is criminal.

➤ If the kissee pulls away, the ladylike or gentlemanly kisser re-
frains from getting mad or pouty. Even if you are dying of humiliation or crying on the inside, maintain a cool and calm
exterior. You can kill yourself later.

➤ When you come up for air and find your mouth poised on the
precipice of their earlobe, proceed with caution and restraint.
Many persons despise ear play all together, on principle, as it reminds them of the wet willies of yesteryear. So go slowly, breathe
softly, blow *ever so* gently, use your tongue sparingly—it should
just delicately graze the outside of the earlobe, not dig for waxen
gold like a Q-tip. If your partner pulls away, do not keep revisit-
ing the area in an effort to convert them.

➤ True ladies and gentlemen are diligent about freshening their
breath. Brush your teeth (and your tongue) often, carry mints
with you at all times, and keep a small tube of toothpaste in your
nightstand drawer for morning touch ups so you—or your partner—
will not have to leave the warm comforts of bed prematurely.

➤ A lady or gentleman *never* goes in for a kiss (or accepts an in-
coming one) during an outbreak of oral herpes. A *true* gentleman
or lady with oral herpes (GoLwOH) explains their situation pre-
kiss even *between* outbreaks. 'Tis true, almost a quarter of the
kissers in this country suffer from oral herpes (most of them un-
knowingly), and yes, the chance of spreading oral herpes *between*
outbreaks is very, very low (especially if you take suppressive medicine). But a true GoLwOH would—and should—still tell. It is only
polite to let your date make their own decision about the risk they
are willing to incur. That said, many a measured gentleman and
lady have been more than understanding when a GoLwOH waited
until the second or third kiss to inform them of the condition. It is

out of our jurisdiction to endorse lies of omission; however, many modern doctors will tell you it is fair play not to tell between out-breaks. A note of caution: This rule does *not* apply to genital her-pes, see p. 197.

<small>✎</small> A lady or gentleman never *expects* a make-out session, or even a good-bye kiss on the lips, at the end of a date. We would do well to remember that kissing is so intimate an act that not even Julia Robert's hooker character in *Pretty Woman* would allow her johns to osculate her. The same thing goes for holding hands in public on a first date, especially before the drinking has commenced. Civilized people find it extremely odd and out of fashion that so many young couples on the show *Blind Date* begin holding hands within the first few minutes of meeting—even when they are not particularly fond of one another. Barbarians, all of them!

For how to cope with bad kissers, see Kiss Off on p. 202.

How to Hickey

The love bite should not be administered (or accepted) willy-nilly. Only the *hidden* hickey (breast, back, shoulder, et cetera) may be given at any time and without permission, assuming the person on the receiving end is thoroughly enjoying it. The half-hidden hickey (e.g., just behind the col-lar) may be administered with *implicit* permission. The blatantly obvious hickey (neck!) may be planted only with explicit permission, or when you know your victim well enough to be sure that it will not get them fired/excommunicated/laughed at for more than a day (and it will not get *you* fired from the relationship).

If you should end up the proud owner of a hickey, do not make a spec-tacle of it (as if it were a new Rolex you purchased on your vacation in the Alps and that you wish to show off to everyone in the office). However, do not exhibit shame merely because you were the privileged recipient of some hot, kinky sex, either. Besides, combing them out does not work, so you will have to wear blemish makeup or a turtleneck—quite a challenge in the midst of a summer heat wave. Simply accept it with grace and move on. If you are a giver, please use discretion; hickeys should not be considered a "patented move," or something you absolutely need to give in order to climax, or anything weird like that. They are an *occasional* gift, like flowers and birthday presents.

If you happen to spot one on someone else, give them the benefit of the doubt and do not be quick to judge, lest you come across as one of those uptight people who always keeps the lights off during sex. However, it is perfectly acceptable to playfully interrogate a colleague about a blatantly obvious hickey. Half-hidden hickeys should be politely ignored by everyone except really, really close friends. The really, really close friend should feel free to ride their hickied pal's ass till the cows come home, but may choose to take the high road because otherwise everyone will know that deep down they are just jealous.

For more on public displays of affection, see p. 62.

 ## SECOND DATES AND BEYOND

This is the infamous period of a relationship after a first date and before "going steady." During this time, you will neglect all responsibilities—to friends, debtors, jobs, family members going in for surgery, houseplants, et cetera, et cetera. You will spend hours prepping for dates (that goes for the gentlemen, too). You will either be a nervous wreck with butterfly-stomach, or else you will have a faraway, dreamy perma-grin on your face as you pretend to listen to your friends' oh-so-mundane tales of work ennui and alligator wrestling. In short, you will be completely and utterly annoying. The lady or gentleman strives to soar above such predictable and plebian behavior.

Making Contact

If the first date goes swimmingly, you would like to see your new friend again, and you are fairly sure they would enjoy your company again also, then by all means mention this at the end of the evening with a carefree yet sincere air about you: You will save them a good twenty-four hours of sweating the phone. Indicate when you will be in touch and stand by this vow. Two to four days is reasonable, though any fop who proclaims that calling the next day is "too keen" should play games in someone else's playground. Well-bred ladies and gentlemen know that the success of adult relationships is not determined by the number of days between a date and a call. That said, it is rude to wait more than four days, unless of course you get hit by a heavy object falling from a great height. Heterosexual ladies would make the world a slightly better place if they took the lead and dialed the digits themselves every once in a while. And if a date says they will call you and fails to do so, chances are they did not lose your number accidentally, and they probably did not get hit on the head by an object falling from a great height either. It is best to simply let it go.

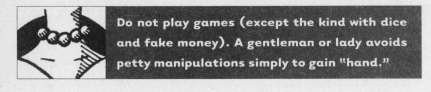

Do not play games (except the kind with dice and fake money). A gentleman or lady avoids petty manipulations simply to gain "hand."

Date Planners

The laziest of daters treats the Moviefone guy like an equal partner in the relationship. But the significance of the phrase "*making* a date" is not lost on true ladies and gentlemen. If making love in the exact same way every time is like a meat cleaver to the neck of your relationship, so too is routine dating. Thoughtful ladies and gentlemen *plan* their quality non-doing-it time. They forgo the dinner-and-a-movie date for something a little more interesting and interactive. They do not attempt to cruise-direct their dates, for they know that flowers, a picnic (complete with actual wicker basket) and a roving mandolin player scream Julie McCoy. (She may have been sexy when you were twelve, dear reader, but no more.) The diligent dater finds a happy medium.

May we suggest subscribing to one of those clever, weekly email newsletters to stay in the loop about local datelike activities? This will assist you in trying without appearing to try *too* hard. In the meantime, we give you some general suggestions below. Simpletons may dismiss them as gouda-esque. However, the wise among us know that if the planets are aligned just so, the chemistry is explosive, you like the way each other's hair smells, and one of you remembered the prophylactics, they may just get you properly laid.

- Seek out a bar or coffee shop with a cupboard full of old-school board games, a shuffleboard table, or bingo nights. A gentleman or lady never lets their date win just to score, as it were, nor does he or she do a little dance when winning. Such uncouth gesticulations betray one's ill breeding.
- Karaoke is not for the faint of heart, so it is prudent to suggest it casually, as a gentle breeze would bring up a few fallen leaves. Have other suggestions in your back pocket. However, should the autumn sun arise in your date's eyes at its mention, then you shall know you have found a kindred spirit. Nothing bonds two souls like crooning an off-key version of "Careless Whisper" together.
- Pay homage to the quaint traditions of yesteryear: Try mini-golf, bowling, or a visit to your local arcade. There is a certain *je ne sais quoi* about the combination of vacation kitsch and high school nostalgia. Plus, it is well-nigh impossible to suck at mini-golf. As for bowling and arcade games, you must rely on natural ability. Remember this, though: being very excellent at either is not necessarily sexy.

➤➤ One-time workshops like a class on wine-tasting or perhaps a seminar on how to shoot porn make for great conversation pieces and bonding experiences. Ballroom dancing classes may be a little intense very early on in a relationship, but if both parties are game (and have rhythm), no need to say no to public, full-body

Persistence vs. Stalking

If you suddenly give her flowers, that is Impulse. If you suddenly give her flowers every morning, that is Persistence. If you suddenly give her flowers every morning with a little note that reads "I love you, you cold-hearted little bitch!" in letters cut out from a magazine you stole from her trash, that, dear friends, is Stalking.

contact. One-on-two tantric instructional seminars are usually best reserved for long-term relationships (see p. 145).

➤➤ Keep an eye out for upcoming concerts in the park, street fairs, walking tours, et cetera. Procure a carriage to the nearest high school make-out point or set up a rustic tent in the rough of your backyard. The constant care of the date planner should be to render the experience agreeable to his companion by the pointing out of any peculiar beauty of the landscape that may have escaped his or her notice, as well as any constellations with which he or she may not be acquainted (that, and making sure both parties don't get eaten alive by bugs or bears). But gentlemen, know this: Making jokes about your "big dipper" is uncouth, not to mention terribly unfunny.

➤➤ Dates are not unlike weddings: None of the traditions are trite when they are happening to you. For this reason, there is nothing wrong with cruising gallery openings and museum exhibits hand-in-hand. Note: A gentleman or lady never refers to a piece of art as "banal" on an early date.

The Ten Commandments of "Seeing" Someone

1. Monogamy is not a monologue; a gentleman or lady never assumes exclusivity until the phrase "Let us refrain from seeing other people" has been uttered. The following are *not* acceptable substitutes: "I really like you"; "Meet my parents"; "Let's do it doggie-style." After the first date and before the first sex, a gentleman or lady may ask, "Are you seeing anyone else?" If the answer is yes, a gentleman or lady will avoid pursuing this line of conversation further (except where matters of safer sex are concerned) unless they're a) Looking for a threeway or b) Missing the jealousy gene. Seeing other people is that person's prerogative—just as it is your prerogative to politely discontinue further dates with them based on this answer.

2. A gentleman or lady does not take advantage of relationship loopholes: If you have been seeing someone for nine months, are celebrating each other's pet's birthdays, and it is abundantly clear your partner assumes monogamy, though you somehow never got around to "The Talk" mentioned in point #1—then you would have to be some kind of uncouth asshole to be participating in extracurricular activities.

3. Expectation management is good manners. A gentleman or lady is gently forthcoming to avoid leading someone on, and says things like "Let's take things slowly/I'm busy all next week/I'm dating a few people right now."

4. It is as rude to leave a letter, email, voice mail, or text message unanswered as it is to leave a question unanswered in conversation.

5. A gentleman or lady may "Google" someone before or after a first date, though we do not recommend admitting to the web

search until the second or third month, when you are in that cutesy "I was so nervous/ excited when I first met you" stage. A gentleman or lady *never* Googles their date's ex.

6. A gentleman or lady is not an oversharer. Subjects that should be approached with extreme caution during the casual "dating" phase include: How to discipline a child, the gory details of past relationships, what you *really* think of their friends, SAT scores, and next summer's vacation plans.

7. Discussing sexual history as it pertains to safer sex is *not* considered oversharing (see chapter VI for more on this). Discussing your last partner's finesse with a buttplug is.

8. Avoid rushing into the long-term, comfortable, "I'm so happy I could fart" stage of a relationship. The early mile-stones of a new coupling—first movie, first kiss, first PDA, first bicker, first roadtrip, first sleepover, first brunch—should be savored and not ingested all at once.

9. A lady knows that most doors are not so heavy that she cannot take her turn holding them open for a gentleman.

Taxi Cab Confession

A gentleman or lady knows that holding open the cab door means their date will be forced to scootch across the entire backseat. A *true* gentleman or lady holds open the door, closes it behind their date, and then walks around the other side to get in. Note to slow walkers: Impatient taxi drivers and busy city streets may cause you to lose track of your date during this maneuver. In this case, either say "I'll get in the other side" to avoid any confusion, or simply get in the backseat first and scootch across. Uncivilized heathens who *think* they are civilized may misinterpret such a move as discourteous. If you suspect your date is one of them, simply explain yourself with a smile as they get in the car huffing and puffing. And if you live in one of those terribly civilized towns where people own houses with driveways and automobiles: A gentleman or lady driver always unlocks and opens the passenger-side door for their guests. Likewise, a gentleman or lady passenger always unlocks the driver-side door after they have been helped into the passenger seat.

10. A gentleman or lady will always steer their date around broken glass, broken sidewalks, dog turds, and doodie in the pool.

Funny Seeing You Here

No matter how modern a lady or gentleman, no matter how forthcoming they have been with each other during the premonogamy phase, nothing is so awkward as to encounter a new friend while out on the town with *another* new friend. How is a gentleman or lady to act in a situation that, on paper, is perfectly legitimate, but in person, feels so odious? Brevity is the soul of good manners at moments like these. A simple introduction ("Walter, this is Edward, Edward, Walter") is the only conversation we can recommend in good faith. Do not attempt to describe the nature of your relationship ("Walter, this is my friend Edward, Edward, this is another of my many friends, Walter"). Simply say, "How are you? Oh, that's great. Well, sadly, we must be going, I'll see you soon," and move on. You will probably find that such an encounter will hasten the monogamy discussion with *both* parties. While you should not feel pressured by this encounter to move into the monogamy phase, you *should* perhaps plan your dates a little more carefully (and discreetly) if this sort of thing befalls you often. And if you should find yourself the odd person out in this scenario, introduce yourself politely to your friend's date, say "How are you? Oh, that's great. Well, sadly, I must be off, I'll see you soon," and move on. Reserve all probing questions for a private conversation later, for purposely making people feel awkward is the antithesis of good manners.

Dinner with Friends

Fresh young couples enjoy congregating almost as much as Grateful Dead fans. These meetings frequently occur at cozy dinner parties. Should you find yourself at dinner with friends, abide by the following rules (in addition to the internationally recognized table manners detailed previously in this chapter):

- When dining over at a friend's, it is a must that you bring some sort of contribution to the evening's festivities, be it a bottle or two of fine vino, a fresh fruit tart for dessert, a tightly packed bowl, or some vintage porn.

- Do not make the host do all the drudge work in the conversation— ask questions, be interested, fake it if you must.

- Always ask the host if there is anything, *anything at all*, you can do to help, even if the game is on. (Do not fret, for they will rarely take you up on the offer.)

- Do not start to nosh until everyone is seated and served; if you are unsure, take the lead from your host.

- There is an old axiom that goes, "Tragedy plus time equals comedy." We would add "Or at least a great dinner-party story." Some stories work over drinks but not food, others work best after midnight, and still others are best kept for immediate family members only. It is basic good manners to be sensitive to your partner's ego and your audience's appetite. Remember, sex can be a fun and spirited topic of conversation so long as the details of the discussion do not embarrass, frighten, publicly out, or betray the confidences of any of the guests.

- Do not leave the table until your host indicates it is time.

- You *must* assist with the clean up. To lazily lounge around by the stereo or play with the Xbox while your host clears the table is terribly rude. And gentlemen would do wise to remember that this is indeed the twenty-first century: Clean up is not the women's duty. If the ladies in your party offer to clean up, it is out of courtesy, not responsibility. Therefore, you should balance the scales by ingratiating yourself during the dish-washing process.

➼ Always thank your hosts, even if you had a terrible time and feel
a case of the runs coming on.

The Art of Being a Nice Guy Who Gets Laid

Being nice is polite, and being polite is sexy. Sadly, a growing number of
heterosexual men complain that women will not date them because they
are "too nice." But being nice is not their problem—*oh no*—whining about
it is. All too often the pathetic, needy, and insecure young men group all
of those traits under the heading "nice" so they may blame their extended dry spell on ladies who dig men behaving badly.

Which is not to say that women do not have a thing for bad boys—but
heed this, readers: They have *flings* with bad boys; they settle down with
nice guys. And in her life, a woman will have many more flings than she
will long-term relationships—so the dating/fucking odds are in favor of
the bad boys. With a fling, qualities like mystery, danger, excitement,
and edge are more appealing than their LTR counterparts: stability, security, and commitment.

However, you *can* incorporate some of those flinglike elements into
regular dating without sacrificing your gentleman status. The key is remembering that when you make it too easy for someone—when you are overly
gushing, dependent, void of any secrets, or even the hint of a dark side—
ladies feel as if they have not earned your affections. Confidence just this
side of cockiness proves that you are with them by choice, not by necessity.

Here is another tip, courtesy of the bad boys: They are not interested
in platonic relationships with women—and they always make that clear.
Nice guys are good friends. But laying down a friendship as the foundation for a romantic relationship can backfire: Once a good friendship is
established, many ladies will not want to risk ruining it by getting gushy.
(At least, that is the excuse they will give you.)

Nice guys often err on the side of consideration. It is an admirable trait, but, while trying to avoid being rude or insensitive, they often come across as indecisive, shy, or pandering. They are not possessed of the audacity, arrogance, or self-centeredness to grab a woman from across the dinner table and plant one on her passionately in the middle of her sentence. Sometimes, that is exactly what a lady wants.

Yet nobody enjoys being treated badly, unless they have more baggage than a Boeing jet and more issues than *Reader's Digest*. What *is* sexy is feeling as if you have converted someone from their bad boy (or bad girl) ways, that the unique healing power of your love has transformed them. It is the typical Hollywood story: longtime cad finally falls for one special person (who, of course, succumbs to a terminal illness). Who would *not* want that fairytale (hold the cancer)?

While good guys often come equipped with a relationship résumé stacked with great references and successful long-term relationships (have you noticed how nice guys are usually friends with their exes?), this does not appeal to many women's desire for a challenge (yes, women are idiots like that, too). They think, "Of course he wants to date me: He is a *dater*." Bad boys with no steady relationships under their belt are like double-dog dares to ladies. They think, "I will not be the first woman this bad boy sleeps with, but I could, perhaps, be the last."

Gentlemen, do not feel the need to align yourself with one group or the other. You should be the best of both: Like Nicholas Cage's character in *Moonstruck*, say, "Now I want you to come upstairs with me and get in my bed!" Just make sure you cook her breakfast in the morning, like any polite gentleman. And remember, what is true of relationships in general is true of sex specifically. Being "nice" does not always mean deep, meaningful, teary-eyed, face-holding "making love." Sex is often hotter when there is a little adversity in the mix, and there is nothing wrong or rude with creating the illusion of adversity to spice up an otherwise "nice" relationship. Take out your frustrations in the sack, use fights to fuel your frolicking, bite, spank. Be a bad boy (or girl) in bed—for that is the only place it counts. See the following chapter for more on "closing the deal."

CHAPTER II
Formal Sex

Many a brute believes the smoothest way to conclude the evening's proceedings is to whip "it" out and ask, "Wanna ride?" Ladies and gentlemen know that more bees are caught with the sweet honey of good manners.

To force or bully someone into bed is not only uncouth, but unconscionable. However, sexual *confidence* can take a lady or gentleman far. There is nothing more attractive than a person who is obviously sexually smitten—and just itching (not literally) to do something about it. Be honest and sincere: Come clean so you can come cleanly. Just remember, there is a fine line between sounding romantic and sounding desperate, between being bold and being a boor. Choose your words carefully, thoughtfully. It is common—and frequently prudent—for ladies and gentlemen to err on the side of caution. Do not, however, mistake spinelessness for politesse. You should be firm and solid, and not so shaky in your confessions that your beloved mistakes you for a bowl of Jell-O.

If you are at all unsure about how to broach the subject, you can kill two birds with one stone by initiating a conversation about sexual histories and recent STD-test results before you get anywhere near the bedroom. Not only will you prove you are responsible and concerned about health and safety, you not-so-subtly convey to the object of your affection that you would like to screw their brains out. Just be careful to avoid sounding presumptuous when you mean to sound courteous and filled with lustful admiration. Do not ever think you are exempt from having the safety discussion: Hubris is one of the greatest risks to your genitalia. (See page 194 for more about STDs.)

When attempting to close the deal, as it were, you may only use the line "Would you like to come up and see my etchings?" if you have *no* etchings. You may only use the term "nightcap" ironically. And you may not automatically assume your date knows that "a drink" (as in "Would you like to come in for a drink?") is code for "a shag that will make the angels weep."

A gentleman and lady never rush. They understand seduction is a dish best served slowly. For the purpose of this point, we shall reluctantly employ a juvenile yet abundantly illustrative analogy: sex as the baseball field. (Hush, gentle reader, and prick up your ears.) There is no need to attempt a home run on the first date. Your chances of getting tagged out while sliding into home plate are greatly reduced with each consecutive date. If you are of a nervous disposition, you would do well to favor a step-by-step process: On the first date, go to first; on the second, go to second; and so on. Regrettably it is not the most original approach, but it is predictable and therefore reassuring. (There will be ample time and suitable opportunity for "unpredictable" on a later date, when you may bring out the gimp.) Please note: If you actually use the baseball metaphor in conversation with the object of your affection, you run the risk of being benched for the season. Like all good ladies and gentlemen, do as we say, not as we do.

Should a lady or gentleman have the good fortune of bedding a new friend on the first date, said lady or gentleman never *ever* assumes that their date is not "relationship material." They understand that to do so would surely disqualify some potentially exquisite relationships with thoroughbred citizens who are perfectly capable of being committed and monogamous. These are evolved members of society who are their own sexual agents, who know what they want, who do not play petty games, and who are independent freethinkers. It is the uncivilized lady or gentleman who believes sex is a bartering tool.

A Note to the Ladies: Do not always rely on the gentleman to make the first move. Life is too short and its opportunities too agreeable for a girl to wallow in other people's sexist traditions. Such blind reliance on these traditions denotes a person who is true to antiquated convention rather than to herself.

ENTERTAINING

When inviting a paramour to one's abode, the gracious host ensures their guest's stay is as comfortable as possible. No need to redecorate; after all, your space is a reflection of who you are—excepting, of course, if you are a filthy pig, in which case betraying yourself and procuring a Swiffer is in order.

Whatever your personality, your bedroom should be a sacred space for rest, relaxation, and rolling in the hay. Any reminders of everyday stresses—CNN on the television, files you brought home from the office, denture glue, stacks of unpaid bills, indeed, your cell phone—can fill your room with negative energy. So get rid of the clutter. You would do well to take note of Hollywood sex scenes—they are lessons in sexual scene setting, with their dramatic, flattering lighting, and soundtracks that create and maintain the mood. (Pay no mind to the fact that they are usually between two Beverly Hills hotties with impossibly perfect bodies in totally unbelievable scenarios.) Everyone has better sex with candles lit and moody tunes on the stereo just loud enough to muffle any accidental, impolite emissions, but soft enough not to disturb the neighbors. It is not at all crass to make a mix CD or cassette for formal boot knocking; it is, however, crass to label it as such. A true lady or gentleman always retires a mix CD after retiring the partner—unless, of course, it is a casual sex mix CD. And do show some restraint with the lighting of candles; more than

Sweet Music for Salacious Times

Etiquette should never be employed to adjudicate matters of taste—except in the case of music played during sex. For if music be the food of love, then R&B is its McDonald's. Yes, Marv and his cronies (Al Green, Barry White, R Kelly, et al.) have made impressive, lucrative careers waxing poetic on the various mountains they would scale and valleys they would traverse for love. And, 'tis true, given enough flutes of champagne, bridesmaids the world over will swoon when the DJ plays "Let's Get It On." But indulge in this soundtrack for sex (or even foreplay) on a regular basis and you risk doing to your libido what so many Big Macs would do to your arteries. This is not to say that R&B is not a wonderful musical genre. It is simply that any-thing that tries too fervently to be sexy is destined for punchline status (witness Geri Halliwell). And even if something starts out auspiciously sexy, once it has been co-opted by the heathen masses or repro-duced enough times, it takes on a patina of cheese. R&B songs have played on too many dancefloors at the end of the night on too many spring breaks; they have even been on the turntable while your parents made their own sweet music. And that Ne-anderthal two cubicles over, the one who dislodges ear wax with his pencil eraser when he thinks no one is looking? He does it to Barry White. These songs are deep-fat-fried in other people's sex lives. They are out of season. Furthermore, there is little worse than being distracted mid-session because you were accidentally singing along. Save "Sexual Healing" for ironic sex.

ten, and you are dangerously close to goth territory. A more subtle approach is to simply dim the lights, or install low-wattage bulbs.

Even more important than atmosphere is cleanliness. There is nothing more inelegant than trying to make love among piles of dirty laundry, an old cereal bowl with curdled milk beside you on the nightstand and a pillow embossed with various Rorschach patterns made in drool framing your face. How pristine you keep your sleeping quarters is suggestive of how you keep your genitals. This correlation will not be lost on your overnight guests. Put them at ease by putting away the clutter and keeping your room clean. The active gentleman or lady always launders the sheets between sleepover guests or every two weeks, whichever comes first.

What is true of your bedroom is doubly so of your bathroom. Stray, wet hairs strewn about the sink and tub are a universal turn-off. Ideally, your guests should feel like they could eat a meal in your bathroom *or* attend to their bodily functions without a care in the world. Napkins or paper towels are no substitute for soft toilet paper: Make sure you always have backup rolls on hand. A box of matches (*not* from Hooters), a votive candle, or an air freshener laid out can be a comforting sight to a guest, even if they have not partaken of the bean dip. However, a gentleman or lady is highly suspicious of anyone who displays a bowl of potpourri in the john. Reading materials in the bathroom should be as at home on your coffee table. In more explicit terms: no skin mags or tasteless joke books (contrary to popular belief, materials featuring potty humor are *not* appropriate). And of the boors who buy toilet paper adorned with golf jokes we cannot even speak. Always have at least one fresh towel and washcloth for each guest, preferably stored in the linen closet; your damp and moldy fourteen-day-old rag should not be shared as a gesture of intimacy. The toilet-bowl lid should always be left down. If that is too taxing, then at least leave the seat down, dear cretin. If there is something you do not want to be discovered—a sex toy, adult diapers, a shrunken head—do not keep it in your medicine cabinet. Finally, as a true lady or gentleman, you should always have a guest toothbrush handy, still in its packaging, just in case a guest requests one. You do *not* keep a drawer full of them for guests to "pick their favorite color," as if you were the sex dentist. Anything that suggests you have a revolving door on your bedroom should be avoided at all costs.

Even if you or your partner uses another form of birth control, and whether or not you are male or female, gay or straight, you should *always* have fresh, quality condoms and/or oral-sex dams on hand, stored in a cool, dry place. Only geezers, sexists, and idiots believe that it is a masculine responsibility. A lady or gentleman takes sole responsibility for their own sexual health.

Your duty as host requires you to be vigilant on a few more matters of decor. One pillow may be sufficient for you, but you should have at least one extra, if not two, for a guest. If you have only one pillow (and really, there is no excuse), then you must give it up to your guest. If you are old enough to be having company over for sex, then you are old enough to have a bed bigger than twin size (no matter if you live in a closet-size studio in New York City). Pictures of exes (innocent or dirty) should be put away out of respect for your guests. If you are currently seeing other gentlemen or ladies, do remember to turn down the volume on the answering machine—you must be honest about your sexual status, but you may never flaunt it. It is not expected, though it is a nice touch, to have quality manmade lubricant on hand—just not in a five-friggin-gallon vat on your nightstand. Keep tissues by the bed for quick clean-ups. And store your condoms discreetly but conveniently. It should go without saying: Leave no opened wrappers—or worse, used rubbers—in sight, even if they are in your wastebasket.

Gentlemen and ladies are like Boy Scouts: They are always prepared. You should be forever at the ready to take on the roles of both gracious host and sex animal. Even if you are suffering a dry spell now measured in years rather than months, that is no excuse for neglecting the duties outlined above and allowing your house to fall into a state of disrepair. You never know when the gods of good manners will shine down on you and reward you with a surprise guest at your door . . . in a uniform . . . with a raging case of nymphomania. That said, we do understand that circumstances may arise that make it nearly impossible to fulfill some of these duties: pets die, earthquakes happen, depression weighs upon us like a debilitating X-ray blanket, the Game Show Network starts replaying your favorite season of "The Price Is Right." If, for whatever reason, your living quarters are serving double duty as a gigantic petri dish growing sundry molds and bacteria, you have three options when faced with the opportunity for sex:

1. Hope your newly found friend suggests their place first. You may *not* invite yourself over to their house. To do so would put your friend in an awkward position of possibly having to deny you. Moreover, you risk characterizing yourself as a leech. The most you may do is regretfully inform them that your home is temporarily uninhabitable. Refrain from going into the gory details of why, but do not be so vague as to allow their imagination to complete the picture (a banana peel rug, a cockroach infestation, inflatable furniture, your significant other). Assuming your "problem" is not a current girlfriend, boyfriend, or spouse, this is one of the few times a small, white lie is acceptable.

2. If it is completely understood and agreed upon by both parties that all intentions are purely carnal (i.e., that neither of you is simply looking for a few more hours of scintillating conversation), then you may, as a bold and romantic gesture, suggest getting a hotel room. You must, however, expect to pay the full price of the room yourself, having made the suggestion. And it goes without saying, the hotel you stay in should be exceptionally cleaner and more comfortable than your home in its current state, lest the point be moot.

3. Tell your special friend you would like nothing more than to whisk them back to your chalet this instant, but you think you should wait and take things slowly. (At least as slowly as it takes to make your manor presentable.) Being—or faking being—a hopeless romantic never goes out of style.

When You Are the Guest

As a guest, you should remember that an invitation to treat someone's body as your own does not automatically mean you may treat their *house* as your own. Act as if your host's living space is a museum until they invite you to do otherwise:

- Leave things the way you found them—especially the toilet seat.
- Please keep your shoes off the furniture. Think about where those soles have been. On the loogie-strewn sidewalks of the world, that's where!
- The habit of biting your fingernails—or, heaven forbid, your toenails—is the height of vulgarity. Nothing is so sickening as to leave behind a souvenir of yourself, so do not do this in public, let alone anyone's bed. If you should catch yourself inadvertently gnawing on them, do *not* fling them behind the head board (or anywhere, for that matter); dispose of them properly and discreetly in a wastebasket.
- When taking a shower, it is polite to ask which products you may use, especially if your lover has a roommate.
- If you do not carry a toothbrush on you (and to do so on nights when you do not have scheduled

A Lover's Best Friend?

Pet owners are earnestly advised not to assume that the love they feel for Fido or Fluffy is shared by the rest of the human race. Nor should they expect a lover to automatically become an animal lover, simply because they themselves have an affinity for Pekinese pups. Such tendencies should be curbed, like one's pets. No matter how much you love your dog or how often said dog serves  as a surrogate bedmate, when you have a homosapien sleepover guest, never assume—or, worse, insist—that your pet join you in the bed. At the *most*, ask if your guest would mind if you have company at the foot of the bed while you sleep. You *must* honor their response—this is nonnegotiable. If you find yourself in the boudoir of a borderline zoophile, you may politely but firmly request that you and your new lover spend the night *alone*. You may even speak of allergies, if need be. If your partner is a person of substance, he or she will make the necessary arrangements for your shared unconsciousness to be undisturbed. If not, may we recommend breaking off the engagement sooner rather than later, for pet fascists do not great lovers make. Of course, if you both happen to be animal people, then you, your lover, and the retriever may happily spoon each other all night long. On a final note, it is unmannerly and unhygienic to kiss one's pets (or anyone's pets) on the lips, especially if you plan on kissing the lips of your sweetheart later that day.

sleepovers would be presumptuous), then ask your host for a spare. If they produce a used one from beneath the sink (and you suspect it may have been used as a cleaning instrument for something other than teeth), you may politely decline and just rinse with toothpaste and water. If, however, they offer you their own brush, it would be impolite to refuse if your tongue has been or is about to be in your host's mouth. Accept it graciously.

➼ Do not cart over items (razor, teddybear, tampons, Playstation, lucky underwear) until specifically invited to do so. And a gentleman or lady avoids leaving items behind "accidentally."

➼ Looking in your host's medicine cabinet is a thing never to be done except in case of necessity. If you are genuinely, indeed *desperately*, in need of something that you do not have on your person, which is not in plain sight, and which you would be mortally embarrassed to ask your host for (e.g., tweezers, cosmetic scissors, razors, Q-tips, pain reliever, et cetera), then you may look quickly, quietly, and discreetly. However, this is not a loophole to be abused. The most highly evolved ladies and gentlemen realize that there is *nothing* more intimate or embarrassing than having sex with someone—not even asking for some Preparation H. Therefore, we recommend being forthcoming over invading someone's privacy. And while we are on the subject, a gentleman or lady never stores their Preparation H behind the mirror.

THE DEED

The Do's and Do Not's of Good and Plenty

Do not make haste. Shooting your wad all at once, so to speak, is indecorous. Sex is not a race, and you are not continually trying to better your time. Besides, it is easier and sexier for your partner to say, "More, harder, O God, faster," than it is to say, "Whoa! Slow down there, cowboy."

Do provide positive reinforcement. To put it delicately, total silence sucks. Your partners will welcome praise and feedback like Mariah Carey would a good review. Plus, it is an easy way to begin dabbling in dirty talk. If you cannot find the words, appreciative noises work just as well.

Do not assume that just because you are in love (or on good behavior), you cannot have it dirty. The idea that marriage, monogamy or even good manners is the end of dirty, throw-me-against-the-wall, taboo-busting sex is a tired, old myth that you should debunk on a regular basis.

However, *do* ask permission before giving your partner a money shot in the face. See p. 114.

Do not keep pushing the idea of a threeway if your partner is decidedly *not* into it. For a threeway to work, everyone has to be whole-heartedly gungho, as well as totally secure, issue-free, and drunk. See p. 92.

Do have an overactive imagination. Talking and fantasizing together about an orgy with your fair mail carrier, your local news anchor, and Notre Dame's coed cheerleading team is usually infinitely more exciting than a real orgy with your hairy, alcoholic, depressed neighbors. Include your partner in your fantasies when it is appropriate. If you are being intimate with them while thinking of someone else, it is usually prudent not to mention it—unless, of course, they are dressed up as that someone else. See p. 132.

Do not become a creature of habit. As Emerson said, a foolish consistency is the hobgoblin of little minds. Be bold and try new things. Your partners will be more receptive to your suggestions if most of those suggestions unselfishly focus on *their* pleasure.

Do practice reciprocity. Do unto others as you would have done unto you. Do not do unto others with the expectation that they must do unto you in return. However, you should assume that when your partner tickles your back, it is not just because they are being nice, but because they would like you to tickle *their* back, too. Finally, if you request something from your partner, you should be able to honor their same or equivalent request without fuss or protest. For example, if you expect your partner's pubic hair to be trimmed like topiary, you should be willing to undergo the same bush trimming. And no knee-jerk reactions to anything as benign as anal penetration, please. See p. 118.

Do not assume that what worked on your previous partners will work on your next one. Everyone is unique. The biggest mistake you can make is arrogantly assuming you know it all. Humility is a sign of a distinguished lady or gentleman.

Do tell your partners what you like; do not expect them to like it, too. There is a difference between having a preference and being a fascist.

Do not pop buttons indiscriminately. Bodice ripping may be sexy in the trashy literature of the day, but it only works in real life when you are confident the item of clothing you are tearing asunder is easily replaceable, not considered a luxury item by your partner, and not an heirloom.

Do remove your socks. Unless your partner specifically requests that you leave them on. A true gentleman will remove his socks as he removes his pants, in one elegant maneuver, to avoid being caught, even momentarily, in a nothing-but-socks moment.

Do not think about baseball just to prolong the inevitable. Being aware of and attentive to others is the cornerstone of good manners. Who desires to fuck someone who is trying to recall all seventy of Mark McGwire's record-breaking home runs in 1998? Only Mark McGwire, that's who. See p. 204 in The Unmentionables chapter.

Do have a sense of humor. There is nothing worse than a serious, sensitive, ponytail gentleman with no sense of irony or the absurd. If you fall off the bed while trying out a new position, do not die of embarrassment—laugh it off and live proudly.

Do not just wash your crotch. Ladies and gentlemen take full baths.

Do wash your hands. Sex is like dining: You should always wash your hands *right* before. If you have been chopping chilis, soap and water will not remove all the oils, so do be careful when you go exploring tender parts with your fingers.

Do not become an obsessive-compulsive cleaner. Natural musky funk is a good thing if your immune systems are compatible—a.k.a., you have chemistry. See p. 182.

Do extend foreplay. A certain amount of teasing is appropriate, especially when it comes to the ladies. There is a time and a place for fevered up-against-the-stairwell-wall sex, but it is usually when you are completely and utterly blotto, at which point good manners are admittedly not a high priority.

Do not misinterpret "no" for "yes" or "maybe." Ever. Honor and respect are what etiquette—sexual and otherwise—is all about. The "butter scene" in *Last Tango in Paris* may be your favorite, but Maria Schneider's no's are fantasy protestations. Those in your own, real-life bedroom are not (unless of course you are participating in a planned BDSM scene and a safeword has been established, see p. 132). Some yahoos may play children's games of coyness, but true ladies and gentlemen know it is of utmost importance to err on the side of caution in such matters. To do anything less is to risk breaking the law and someone's spirit, to say nothing of ruining your reputation.

Do make eye contact. To avoid it screams that you are either afraid of intimacy, that you are thinking of someone else, or that you think your partner is hideous.

Do not answer phone calls. Not only is it disrespectful to your partner to interrupt your lascivious interlude (as if anything is more important than lovemaking), but it is rude to the poor soul on the other end of the line who has now been unwittingly incorporated into your session.

Orgasm Etiquette

Modern ladies and gentlemen know *one* partner's orgasm is not the finishing tape of a sex run. Think of the romp as a three-legged race—your partner can neither compete nor cross the finish line without your help, and vice versa. Each partner makes a concerted effort to satisfy their partner before the towel is thrown in.

Let us first turn to the matter of heterosexual couples' orgasms. The idea that a so-called gentlemen does his business and then turns over to go to sleep is as outmoded as snuff. In fact, in this day and age, it is courteous for both parties to attempt to evoke at least one orgasm from the lady first. Because a woman's post-orgasmic resolution phase is slower and more gradual than a man's, she can often continue to receive and enjoy stimulation, including penetration, long after her first O; indeed, such continued attention may result in multiple orgasms for a few lucky bitches . . . excuse us, *ladies*. In contrast, men who have climaxed first may consequently struggle against their own quicker resolution and its attendant urges toward sleep and television watching. However, this is no excuse for shirking sexual responsibility. Men can and should continue to pleasure their female partner until she is satisfied (whatever satisfied means to that individual).

A word of caution, though: The only thing worse than a man who does not care about a woman's orgasm is one who cares about it to the exclusion of all else. This is the man who heads downtown and vows not to come up for air until his girlfriend does her best Meg Ryan. He approaches handwork like weeding ("Must. Dig Up. Orgasm!") and swears, in dulcet tones an octave lower than his usual voice, that he is dedicated to "female pleasure." He wants to be a super-lover—his ego depends upon it. He covets her orgasms like a Boy Scout covets merit badges. While the intention is indeed admirable, all that pressure can leave a lady wishing she had just played croquet instead. Furthermore, giving her performance anxiety is the best way to ensure she will not reach orgasm. Attentive gentleman, fret not, for you will not lose your "Sensitive Guy" merit badge if you believe her when she says that she is delighted with the sex for sex's sake, and give up graciously. Sometimes the fat lady simply will not sing. But that does not mean everyone cannot still enjoy the show.

Of course, straight ladies are not the only ones whose orgasms occasionally go missing. Lesbians and men (both gay and straight) are mere mortals, too. 'Tis true, sapphists are freed from the limitations of the male model of doing it and therefore can often provide each other more physiologically and psychologically appropriate stimulation for the female orgasm. And yes, men's equipment is fairly straightforward and therefore more easily manipulated. However, factors that may inhibit "the little death"—dry skin, urge to pee, spinning room, trouble at the office—are not always discriminating. And of course there is always a chance that—stop the presses!—*he* might not be in the mood.

No matter who you are, if you find yourself clinging to the cliff's edge, unable to let go, never apologize. Do not throw a fit like a frustrated child. Do not blame your partner or yourself for this perceived "failure"; so long as you both have enjoyed yourselves, and have not frightened the horses, there is only success. Most importantly, do not fake it. Many ladies and gentlemen (yes, *gentlemen*), with only the best intentions, think an Oscar-winning performance is good manners. However, like any deception, this leads to no good. You may ultimately find yourself backed into an orgasmless corner, forced to keep up the charade because of your partner's heightened expectations, unable to openly explore different techniques with them that may ultimately work. Everyone needs their little secrets, but ones about your sexual needs should not be kept from your lover. As long as you sincerely express your thorough enjoyment of your partner's oral acumen or anal ability, there is no need for garish displays of false ecstasy. Should you find yourself witness to a ruse, we suggest that you play along. To call "bullshit" on a partner who felt the only decent, indeed, the only *polite* thing to do was moan wolf is the equivalent of a slap in the face with a pair of white gloves—it is only done these days by boors.

But what if you cannot decipher whether their "Oh, yeah, oooh, uh, more, oh, shit, yeah, baby, fuck!" is an expression of thorough *orgasmic* enjoyment or simply thorough enjoyment? While you may not harp on the matter or make it a topic of conversation *throughout* your session, it is not impolite to ask your partner, after the conclusion of your romp, if they came. After all, people's orgasms come in all manner of shapes, sizes, and expressions. Inquiring as to your partner's *petit mort* reflects a caring about their satisfaction, and may help you better provide for them in the future. You may not, however, under any circumstances, inquire "How was it for you?" Such clichés are never to be indulged in.

Let us say you find yourself opposite someone you are *certain* has not O'ed, despite your best efforts. Do not take it personally. Do not call your partner "frigid"—such expressions reflect a complete lack of understanding and education on your part. Do not suggest that your partner's equipment is faulty or "aging." To make your partner feel guilty, silly, or abnormal is rude beyond forgiveness, and only speaks to your insecurities and ill-breeding. You may, at most, speak in positives, just touching on your desire to please them *more* at a later date—all the while conveying what a good time you have had.

If you yourself have the good fortune of climaxing, know that there is no greater ornament to an orgasm than a heartfelt moan or sigh. Like applause from the grateful audience at an orchestra performance, any vocalization of your pleasure will be appreciated by sensitive partners. And when a lady or gentlemen does *you* the honor of orgasming (or even just thoroughly enjoying themselves sexually) in your presence, take it with an air of grateful deference to demonstrate your appreciation of that honor. Under no circumstances may you make fun of someone's orgasmic style, the funny faces or queer noises they may uncontrollably emit. A lady and gentlemen are never more beautiful than when they are in the throes of orgasmic bliss, even if they are whinnying like an ass. For more on orgasm awkwardness, see p. 204.

A Note to Overachievers: The simultaneous orgasm is rarer than good manners at an Irish pub after last call. If it should happen, chalk it up to serendipity and consider yourself blessed. But do not chase it like a pot of gold at the end of a rainbow.

Post Sex

A good cuddle after a vigorous mating ritual is what separates us from the animals. To suggest that you have personal space issues or are sensitive to overstimulation *after* you have had your anus tongued is vulgar behavior suited only to fishmongers. A minimum of fifteen minutes of quality embracing/back tickling/hair tousling is in order, no matter how tired or full of remorse you may be. If you happen to be partial to cuddling, never expect or demand that it exceed an hour.

Intricate Dance of the Wet Spot

No civilized woman or man should be subjected to the discomfort and humiliation of sleeping in the wet spot, no matter if he or she is the source of the deluge. If the bed is big enough, sleep around it. It is the host's responsibility to procure a clean towel or blanket to put over the "damn spot" and offer to sleep on it; in fact, the host should insist on sleeping on that side. If there are no extra linens and the bed is small, both partners should share the burden of the wet spot and switch places regularly until it is dry.

The If we are talking about evening, late night, or early morning encounters of the intimate kind, the *truly* civilized will expect the cuddling phase to automatically progress into the sleepover phase, without fretting over the implications—for there are none. Well-bred ladies and gentlemen know that sharing unconsciousness is not necessarily a symbol of commitment or love, it is simply a nice thing to do. It is the hardcore fucking that has the messy implications.

If you are the host and the sun has already set, you may ask your date to vacate the premises *only* in case of emergencies: your parents are visiting early the next morning, you suffer from a sleep apnea disorder, your house is on fire. Other than that, if it is midnight and you are spooning naked in bed, it is polite to suggest, during the cuddling, that your party stay the night. If you have reservations about them sleeping over *before* you have the sex, then may we suggest you keep your trousers on; *after* the sex, you have no option. A gentleman or lady always offers coffee the next morning. If the cupboards are bare, it is nice to suggest heading out for brunch. Finally, as the time for their departure nears, a host's relief at the prospect is not to be revealed until after the guest has taken their leave. The final cheek kiss good-bye is to be performed with the same warmth as the first tongue hello. *Especially* if you suspect this is the last time you will ever see them.

If you are someone's guest, and you have an early wake-up call, you are allergic to your date's cat, or you think you may have left the stove on, you may politely excuse yourself, though a thorough explanation for and demonstration of regret over your departure is required. Should your host fail to extend you a formal invitation to stay over, it is correct to assume the invitation is implicit. After fifteen minutes of cuddling, if your host turns his or her back on you in order to sleep, you must respect this decision and stay on your side of the bed. Come morning, a gentleman or lady does not outstay his or her welcome. In the first month of a relationship, one should depart as soon as the crossword has been completed, assuming you can finish it before three o'clock in the afternoon. (However, if you decide to continue spending time together off-site, as it were, there is no specific deadline for taking your leave.) And yes, dear readers, tipping is always inappropriate, no matter how good the oral was.

Kissing and Telling

It is often said that ladies and gentlemen do not kiss and tell. And for the most part, they do not. What lady and gentleman would follow up an afternoon tryst with a press release? However, the undeniable, simple joys of a good, discreet, dish session prevent us from passing on this edict without qualification. Prudence advises you to choose one—at most, two—good friends whom you trust with your scuttlebutt. A one-night stand with someone outside your social circle is fair fodder for a slightly wider audience, as are generic and complimentary comments ("It was the best missionary sex I have ever known!"). Negative comments about your partner's performance (size, stamina, creativity, et cetera) should only be shared with one, intimate, tight-lipped acquaintance. The same applies to particularly kinky minutiae.

One of the greatest misconceptions of this century is that locker-room talk only happens in the male changing rooms. To be sure, the men who walk among us are generally more proficient at retelling a dirty joke. But when it comes to dirty stories—the sordid, steamy, and especially the humiliating details about last night—the ladies dominate. Though we are loathe to curtail a woman's public embrace of her sexuality, she would do well, at times, to take heed from gentlemanly prattle. If a man has great casual sex, he will describe it thus: "Yeah, we did it." If he is the verbose type, he might add that "she was up for anything." If he has mediocre casual sex, he might say, "I'm so hungover." If a man has great sex in a long-term relationship, he will say he is in love. And if he has mediocre sex in a long-term relationship? He will never speak of it. Women, on the other hand, can be worse than Tolkien when it comes to belaboring a point. Every dirty word her partner utters in the heat of the moment, every finger he pokes in the wrong place, every inadvertently funny facial expression he makes, all is dished up with relish. But it is only the vulgarians who believe that just because it happened on *Sex and the City*, it is appropriate behavoir.

As a general rule, the more serious a relationship becomes (and therefore the more time your partner spends with your friends), the less appropriate all this salacious chin wagging becomes. Not that it is necessary to renounce it completely, of course—our friends and neighbors are an invaluable source of sexual education, and we would be fools to pass up this opportunity to learn from one another (and in this matter, gentlemen would do well to emulate the ladies a little more often). It is a simple matter of politesse to consider whether your friends would enjoy your dinner parties more if they knew a little less about each other's butt-plug proclivities. Finally, it is unspeakably rude, on myriad levels, to exaggerate one's stories to improve their narrative tension or climax, so to speak. Such embellishment nulls any educational benefit of the tale, creates false envy or even feelings of inadequacy in your audience (if not suspicion), disrespects your partner and, most disconcertingly, makes a liar out of you.

SPECIAL OCCASIONS AND SITUATIONS

PDA and Public Sex

What, pray tell, could be vulgar about the expression of love? Nothing, so long as that expression is conducted in private. Once you step outside, you must take into consideration the delicate sensibilities of all the puritanical plebes who inhabit this fair land—it is the only polite thing to do.

As far as public displays of affection go (also known as PDA), couples are encouraged to hold hands, kiss *without* tongue, and make lovey-dovey eye contact with abandon (assuming they are neither in church nor at work, nor in the company of a recently heartbroken friend). Kissing with tongue in public is to be avoided except at airports and train stations—assuming your beloved will be gone for more than a weekend. An occasional pinch of the buttocks is acceptable, though the intent should be whimsical and jocular rather than salacious. Genitals and breasts should never be pinched or fondled in public.

Now, as for secret sex in public places, that is a puzzling labyrinth of sexual etiquette. As long as you remain undiscovered, you do not force your coitus onto unsuspecting passersby, and you avoid frightening the horses, then it is perfectly acceptable. But by definition, public sex includes the perpetual danger of being discovered. Indeed, not being able to control your surroundings is its appeal, a part of its thrill. Unfortunately, bringing people unwittingly into your sick and twisted perversions is perhaps one of the rudest things you can do: the ultimate imposition. For though your partner may think it fine and dandy, most other people do not want to see your pasty ass. Therefore, public sex can become un-mannerly in the blink of an eye—*literally*. You must calculate the risks of discovery and proceed accordingly. Use the chart on p. 64 to determine when and where sex in public spaces is, in fact, kosher. In all cases, it should go without saying, you must not leave behind any evidence of your salacious activities (condoms, sticky seats, et cetera).

On a final note, should you be discovered in the act of public sex, it is unthinkably churlish to close your eyes or merely stay frozen and pretend you are invisible. If your accidental intruder is a civilized being, he or she will move on quickly and allow you to continue in congress. If, however, the intruder is unable to move on (due to a seating assignment, traffic jam, or digestive emergency, et cetera) you must, as they say, get a room. You may only continue if your onlookers are far enough away that they can discern the act but not the actors (e.g., you are on a roof and they are four buildings over). And should you accidentally turn a private sexual session into a public one by, for instance, walking into a room you thought was unoccupied, run away.

As far as indecent exposures go, one should avoid dabbling in public nudity—be it streaking, mooning, flashing, or wearing Speedos—unless one is at a nude beach, at college, or in Europe.

Coworker Sex

Sneaking to the fax room on your lunch break . . . leaving dirty Polaroids under each other's keyboards . . . doing it on your boss's desk while he or she is at the Hamptons . . . Dipping your pen in the company inkwell may not be exactly *encouraged* in the modern workplace, but most people who consider themselves ladies and gentlemen have dipped at least once. It used to be that love on the clock was for executive married men and their young female secretaries only; the greatest concern was that in a fit of

THE PUBLIC SPACE	IF YOU ARE A COUPLE	IF YOU ARE ALONE
Airplane lavatory	The urbane lady or gentleman knows that the space constraints of coach lavatories, despite their mythic status, make sex next to impossible, not to mention terribly uncomfortable. Let us not go into the unsanitary conditions that are not even suitable for bodily functions, let alone sex. However, in first-class johns, anything goes.	As long as you do not hold up the line, diddle away.
Airplane seat, under a blanket	Only if there is no one sitting next to you, or in the same row across the aisle. You must wait until the meal has been served, the crew has turned off the main cabin lights, and the feature presentation has begun. It is also your responsibility to keep a watchful eye out for flight attendants, and you must stop whenever one approaches.	Same as couple.
Under a dinner table at a restaurant	Only if the tablecloth almost reaches the floor, and you can perform your techniques with a bare foot. But you must not suffer from pungent foot odor, lest you upset the other diners' appetites.	For a couple, this is perverse yet romantic. For a lone diner, it is simply perverse.
In a car	Only at deserted dead ends and make-out points. If you are on an old-fashioned double date, both parties must be willing to engage in equivalent sexual acts, lest one couple is forced to engage in awkward small talk while the other performs the "two-humped dromedary." We cannot condone high-speed handjobs or oral administrations	Same as couple. Be sure you are not parked within a school-safe zone.

THE PUBLIC SPACE	IF YOU ARE A COUPLE	IF YOU ARE ALONE
	due to the increased risk of accidents, which is pretty much the height of rudeness to other drivers.	
At the office	Only after hours. You may do it in any public office area, in your own work area, or in the work area of anyone above you in the corporate hierarchy. It is discourteous to do it in the work area of anyone who reports to you or is a peer.	Anywhere, anytime, as long as there is a lock on the door or your colleagues are mannered enough to *always* knock.
In a public bathroom	As long as it is a single bathroom with a lock on the door and there is no one waiting in line. You must finish your business within three minutes of the first knock on the door	Same as couple.
In an alleyway	You must stay standing and should pull clothes aside rather than removing them. If you are caught by someone who claims the alley as a home, you must donate at least five dollars to their cause and move on quickly.	This is simply too depressing to dignify with a comment.

jealousy, said secretary would know exactly how to contact the missus. Nowadays, fortunately and felicitously, dating in the workplace requires a whole new set of etiquette rules.

Before soliciting a coworker, a gentleman or lady considers the matter in the same way he or she would ponder approaching a bartender at their local: Am I prepared to drink elsewhere if it all goes pear-shaped? Chances are, within a few months, your coconspirator will have moved on romantically, or simply will not care. (Do we all not have at least one ex in our circle of friends?) The decision will depend on the happy-hour specials or holiday bonuses, as well as on the potential of the relationship. You risk less for a one-night stand than for a chance at true love, which comes along less often than a charming little watering hole or a decent job offer.

Should you decide the risk is worth taking, then you will most certainly have to set some boundaries and come to a few understandings. For example: What happens outside of work, stays outside of work; there will be no abuse of power, no sexual harassment, and no sexual-harassment lawsuits; there will be no special treatment or undeserved promotions; when you meet up after work, there will be a set deadline at which point all shoptalk must cease, et cetera. Of course, as you cannot predict the erratic behavior of the psychotic coworkers you choose to bed, you can only be responsible for your own good behavior and pray for the best. Again, dear friends, that is the risk of mixing business with pleasure.

When it comes to coitus with a cubicle colleague, the secrecy is undeniably at least half its provocative appeal. Obviously, there are myriad reasons not to dispatch a company-wide memo after the first interlude: If it ends within two weeks, you do not want everyone else feeling awkward; it is infinitely easier to abscond to the copier room for a quickie if no one suspects your motives; perhaps it is frowned upon by your HR department; perhaps you are new at the company and do not want your reputation marred early on; or maybe you do not want all the office gossips spying on those awkward first few conversations at the water cooler. The most important

Go with the Flow Chart

We must insist that you interpret the term "coworkers" literally. Sex between a boss and his or her underling involves far too many  messy power dynamics that invariably get abused. And let us not forget the inevitable resentment such insider trading stirs among the staff members who choose to keep their pants on. Stick with someone on the same rung of the corporate ladder. Even more fortuitous if they are in a different department.

reason, of course, is that true ladies and gentlemen never kiss and tell in situations in which to do so would embarrass the protagonist of the tale or potentially harm (or at least alter) their professional reputation.

However, you cannot expect to keep the affair clandestine forever. At some point (usually after three to six months), you must acknowledge whether it is just the secrecy that is sexy, or if true feelings have developed in one or both parties. If those involved have conflicting expectations, termination is the only honorable thing to do. If both parties are on the same page, then they may proceed as desired. Should a serious relationship be budding, there is no need to hide the affair. However, when the cat is finally out of the proverbial bag, do not, under any circumstances, make out or—worse—call each other by pet names in front of coworkers. Such familiarity in professional spaces will arouse their contempt, if not their lunch.

When using the clever enter-the-office-at-different-times ruse, place more than two minutes between entrances. Coworkers are not as mentally challenged as you might think.

Roommate Sex

For those ladies and gentlemen with a roommate, the when, where and how of sex can be difficult to negotiate. As tempting as it may be, you may not copulate in shared spaces or on public furniture—for example, the chaise longue in the living room, the kitchen table. The shower and bathtub, however, are acceptable staging areas because of their built-in clean-up features and the nature of bathrooms in general (i.e., dirty things happen behind locked potty doors). It should go without saying that your roommate's bed is strictly off-limits. If, heaven forbid, you share a bedroom with someone, then you may not have sex in the room while your roommate is sleeping; you may do so only if they are passed out drunk. If you have the good fortune of having separate bedrooms, then make sure you close your bedroom door behind you and keep your howls of ecstasy at a low volume. If your roommate is having sex behind his or her closed door, do not disturb them; even if their cooing is keeping you up, to intrude is a punishment that does not fit the crime. Plug your ears and wait until morning when you can politely ask your roommate, in private, that he or she respect your boundaries. And if you are having sex with your roommate, then God help you, for no amount of etiquette will save you from the inevitable blow up.

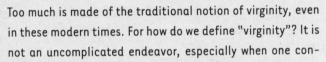

VIRGIN TERRITORY

Too much is made of the traditional notion of virginity, even in these modern times. For how do we define "virginity"? It is not an uncomplicated endeavor, especially when one considers Mother Nature's fondness for diversity. Sex is not only vaginal penetration with a penis, it is a great blowjob in the back of a Honda, it is the delicate fingering of one young lady by another, it is mutual masturbation between boyfriends, it is reciprocation, it is true love. For our purposes here, let us assume, like all thoughtful ladies and gentlemen, that virginity is in the eye of the beholder. Whatever you may consider the ultimate act—be it oral, vaginal, or anal penetration with a finger, a tongue, a penis, or a dildo, or even just frottage to the point of climax— *that* is what we mean by "virginity." To limit our view of sex and its infinite possibilities only serves to limit our pleasure.

However it is defined, losing one's virginity is a momentous occasion, whether at thirteen or at thirty. Even if the day comes when we cannot recall all the names of everyone we have known biblically (forsooth, we may not even remember all the *faces* of the people we have known biblically), we will *always* remember our first—from the time of day to the weather outside, from the unfortunate tune playing on the stereo to the actual physical feeling, whether pleasurable or painful. For this reason, doing it "right" is even more important. All sex should be approached with a modicum of respect, but especially virgin sex. No doubt a lack of respect may make for great "crazy" first-sex stories, but they only become great and crazy after much time and distance—in the moment they are simply traumatic and depressing, and will shape (read: fuck up) the way we think of sex for years to come. Too many people report, with an unconvincing smile and shoulder shrug, that their first time was awkward and unsatisfying, just something to be gotten over with. But it does not have to be that way; a good time *can* be had. If you appreciate the magnitude of the event, then you can help make it nice. And is that not what etiquette is all about—making nice?

For Cherry Poppees

All virgin gentlemen and ladies should report their sexual status to their partners *before* those partners, unbeknownst to them, change that status. As is almost always the case with sex and etiquette, honesty is the best policy. Many polite virgins fear that a confession will upset their partners and scare them off, leaving the virgins with their flowers *still* intact. However, any person worth their sex would be utterly delighted at the prospect of fresh meat to sculpt and mold into their ideal lover. If they are bright, they will think, "I am the best lover my partner has ever had!" Because they *are*. Besides, it will only benefit you to give them the opportunity to make it as agreeable for you as possible. If you are giving your V-card to someone with manners, they will *want* to do this for you. Assure them that you will not expect a ring and eternal devotion simply because they are going where no one has ventured before.

Go slowly. Breathe. Relax. And that is just when you are telling them the good news. Do the same when you do the deed. Do not worry if the earth does not move the first time, for every new sexual embrace only gets better with practice. And remember, you are entitled to have sex the way you want, not the way your teachers (those who may not be virgins) tell you it should be. Just because you have never done it before (whatever "it" means to you), does not mean you do not know the right way to do it. The right way to do it is the way that feels good to you, so long as it does not hurt or humiliate your partner or frighten the horses.

There is one thing that should always be remembered by those who are virgins, which is this: Just because you have never had sex before does not mean you are exempt from following the rules of sexual etiquette. Do not use your inexperience as an excuse for rude/boorish/inappropriate/selfish behavior. Even if you are nervous and ever so slightly "freaking out," behave—it will give you a sense of control and help make things go as smoothly as can be expected.

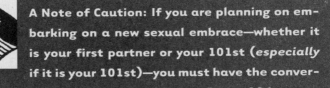

A Note of Caution: If you are planning on embarking on a new sexual embrace—whether it is your first partner or your 101st (*especially if it is your 101st*)**—you must have the conversation about each other's sexual history. See p. 194.**

See p. 194.

For Cherry Poppers

The onus is on you to make this a positive experience. It is quite a hefty responsibility, but also an honor, not unlike being someone's best man or maid of honor. You have been chosen to fill this one position in someone's life, and there will be no others (unless, in the former case, they get divorced and remarry or, in the latter, join a weird cult and become a born-again-virgin).

Every well-bred man and woman knows that a flair for romance, a dedication to communication, and an appropriate sense of humor are imperative in polite cherry popping. Do not judge a fledgling's fumbling performance, do not call them names such as "Two Pump Chump," and certainly do not point and stare, or worse, laugh. Few other sexual circumstances require the virtue of patience as much as this (except perhaps if you are dealing with limp dicks or premature ejaculators, see p. 204).

Remember to let your virgin set the pace. If they are bucking like a mechanical bull, you may gently suggest alternative approaches. But if it is not uncomfortable to you and they seem to be thoroughly enjoying themselves, you must forgive them this lack of grace, for you can always instruct them on the ways of love at a later date. (See p. 200 for how to make a bad lover better.) If your virgin is hardly moving and you are doing all the work, ask them if you may continue, if they would like to go slower or faster, if they would prefer that you stop, if they would like to take a snack break. Do not be or act surprised if this rite of passage loses its charm for them after approximately five minutes, especially if nothing multiorgasmic is happening: Like New Year's Eve, the reality does not always live up to the hype.

Most important, look your virgin in the eyes. Not only will that help you determine how they are doing, it will make them realize that for you, being a cherry popper is more than a duty—it is a delight!

To be sure, this is not a relationship to be entered into lightly or breezily. If you have any reservations about taking on this responsibility, or feel you are not up to fulfilling the duties required of a cherry popper, then best to step down and move on. (And do not be embarrassed about confessing to these reservations; it is no more a failure than to request a seat reassignment upon finding yourself in the emergency-exit row on an airplane.) You would do well to remember that we humans—especially the virgins—have an amazing capacity to convince ourselves that things are the way we *wish* they were. We like to interpret actions—the way you hold our hand in the movies, the way you spontaneously kiss us on the forehead and tell us we are so precious, the way you email us first thing every morning—as confirmation that you have been converted to the cult of commitment, no matter what you have actually *said*. It is imperative that you balance your actions with open communication. You of course are not required to fall in love with your virgin. However, if you are not serious about your snow-white lily, and have no intentions of sticking around to help them refine their rough sexual technique, then this must be laid out on the table. Anything less would be downright barbaric.

And should the news of your partner's virgin status take you by surprise, do not automatically assume they will accept nothing less than true love and start running for the hills. Virginity does not have to be a deal breaker. Again, approach them with appropriate respect and sensitivity, as you would any person, and the rest will fall into place. Virgins are people, too.

For Poppers and Poppees Alike

While it is encouraged that you set the mood for any sex, it is imperative that you do so for first-time sex. You may indulge in all the crazy, dirty, public-bathroom sex you would like, *later*. For this singular occasion, let us think: time, space, quiet. You may make farm animal noises until the proverbial cows come home, but limit any outside distractions. Turn off your cell phones (*always* a polite pre-sex gesture) and make sure neither of you has to rush off to any subsequent engagements. Dim the lights enough so you both look more attractive than you really are, but not dim enough so you cannot see each other. And again, choose your soundtrack carefully: Nothing too crass, such as Lil' Kim or Peaches, but nothing overly sentimental such as Julio or Enrique, lest you inadvertently make such sap "your song."

It cannot be too strongly impressed upon ladies and gentlemen that protection always be used. Those who are "technically" virgins are not immune to the plagues of the genitals, for they can certainly pick up uninvited viruses, parasites, and bacteria by simply bumping uglies externally with another. And the "experienced" partners may not be as

educated as they would like to believe. Just because they have never noticed any problems down below does not mean they are free and clear—
many STDs can be asymptomatic, and people (especially men) are often
just *carriers* of infections that can royally offend their partner's unsuspecting genitals. We must also suggest a backup method of birth control
as a thoughtful cautionary measure. (See p. 194 for more on these sensitive issues.)

When you pick up the condoms and/or oral sex dams (and once again:
you are *both* responsible), it is a nice gesture to purchase some lubricant,
too. This is not cheating, it is simply (im)moral support. Whether you have
rutted once or a thousand times, lubricant can make everything more
comfortable and give you both a smoother ride—for wet is sexy. Thoughtfulness will help you avoid irritating someone's delicate sensibilities *as
well as* their delicate physical being: Select water-based lubes without
glycerin (which can cause yeast infections in women) or nonoxynol-9 (which
can irritate some vaginas and anuses).

When you are in the middle of this momentous lascivious encounter,
do not rush the curtain call. The mentor in this scenario should not
expect—or even try—to achieve their own climactic ending during the de-
flowering act. At the very least they must wait until after the V-card has
been confiscated. However, the most sensitive and gracious ladies and
gentlemen will put their own pleasure and satisfaction on the shelf in order to pay full respect and homage to the soon-to-be ex-virgin. It should
go without saying that the ingenue should not be made to feel a failure if
they fail to climax.

Finally, after it is all over, we must insist that you cuddle—twice as
long as you normally would. Spend the rest of the day/night together. For
if you follow all of the above etiquette, you shall both be wanting to do it
again before day's end.

Special Considerations If Your Virgin Is a Maiden and Sex Means Penetration

If we are talking about penetrative intercourse, then we are talking about preparation. Considering a lady's anatomy and sexual response, first-time sex is not just a simple matter of inserting, swirling, and repeating—not if you would like her to truly enjoy herself, as all courteous people do.

- **Begin with manual labor.** Gradually work your way up to sausage size over several sessions with first one, then two, three, even four fingers.

- **Do not forget the warm-up act.** We are quite sure we are preaching to the choir here, but for those of you just learning how to walk upright: Foreplay is always important, but it is *most* important immediately before a lady loses it. Teasing can be a most agreeable way to relax all the vaginal muscles and get her juices flowing (a most indelicate phrase, to be sure). So once you have both decided that "tonight's the night," make her wait for it so long she will wonder if you are reneging. Of course, getting her in the mood may not be an option, depending on how nervous she is. If she is lying on her back staring at the ceiling, legs akimbo and fists clenched, yelling "Damn you, just get it over with!" then it is polite to move things along.

- **Go slowly.** Infinitesimally slowly. More slowly than you think you should. Gently press in one's peter about a quarter of a centimeter then gently pull back. Gently press it in again about a half-centimeter then gently pull back. And so on and so forth and yet again . . . In fact, this is quite a nice technique to revisit in the future, virgin or no virgin.

- **Multi-task.** Stimulate her other erogenous zones for a pleasant Pavlovian effect. Just because this event is mostly about her vagina, do not leave her clitoris stranded on the side of the ballroom with an empty dance card.

- **No jackhammering.** Again, this is good manners no matter who you are doing. Yes, some ladies like it, but more than ten minutes of getting genitally punched like a boxing bag never got any lady off—*especially* virgin ladies.

Special Considerations If Your Virgin Is a Chap

Do not be late for the appointment.

CHAPTER III
Casual Sex

It was at one time the fashion to affect a certain negligence toward casual sex, which was known in the vernacular as "free love"—or, more commonly, "free love, man"—and was supposed to be the result of a higher state of sexual being. This kind of congress (be it a tête-à-tête, three's company, or one grand love-in) was famously unencumbered by tedium—no conventions, no expectations, no phone numbers, no worries. Nowadays, it is perfectly acceptable to look back on these times fondly, as one regards a decades-old tie-dye tee in the back of a dresser drawer—both are rich with the comforting scent of sentimentality. But the modern lady and gentleman know that this approach to casual sex is decidedly outmoded. In spite of its informality—or perhaps because of it—casual sex requires basic principles of conduct just like any other brand of coupling. To assume otherwise would be as gauche as wearing sweats instead of khakis on casual Fridays.

By "casual" sex, we mean to say that it is acceptable to check your emotions at the door and treat the comingling as a mostly physical event; we do not mean that there are no rules or consequences. Besides, if friendly lust-making is simply a pleasant way to pass an evening— along the lines of, say, charades—why not treat it like any other game? We do not object to rules in chess or croquet; it would be boorish to find fault with them in the bedroom (or in the dive-bar bathroom). Far from impinging on the merriment, rules simply lay down the mundane details so you can better enjoy the intricacies of the game, whatever kind of field you find yourself in (and with however many players).

It should hardly be necessary for us to say that modern ladies find casual sex agreeable as often—perchance more often—as do modern gentlemen. And unlike in days of old, these ladies no longer harbor a secret hope that the salacious encounter will lead to something more permanent—at least the well-bred ladies do not. It would not be erroneous to say that some of them do not even expect dinner. Like the gentlemen who came before them (though one would hope not *literally*), they understand that sex need not always mean the same thing, and sometimes it need not mean a thing at all. Which is not to say that deep, meaningful, soul-melding orgasms are out of fashion—rather, sometimes a lady or gentleman simply wants to get off. Sex can be recreational, a learning experience, a practice session, a boredom reliever, an ego boost—and unlike croquet, no one has to lose (and errant balls are less likely to cause injury). A woman accomplished in this *beau art* may choose to consummate a casual encounter not because she hopes a gentleman will return her affections, but rather because she is ambivalent on the matter. We are amused to note that the women often *do* enjoy their casual sex unencumbered. Rarely do the latchkey ladies have to face the dreaded inquiry, "When will I see you again?"—because the gentlemen, oblivious to the ladies' self-interests, are too busy planning their own discreet exit.

Part of the appeal of casual sex for the ladies of today lies in the hint of anonymity it affords. It grants them permission to be whomever they wish. Freed from the burden (if we may call it a burden) of making a gentleman fall in love with her, she is at liberty to focus on the act itself, without messy emotions impeding an agreeable time. If she is the kind of lady who typically concerns herself with decorum, with airs and graces, with old-fashioned notions of what a lady does and does not say—she can leave all that baggage at the door with the butler. She is free to frolic, to fulfill her basic sexual needs (forsooth, the ladies have them, too). Perhaps raised to be a giver, she can finally take. She can be what we like to call a "selfish lay." She can conduct herself in what might be termed—by persons who hold stock in such gender stereotypes—a *gentlemanly* fashion.

Those of you familiar with the infinitely malleable "science" of evolutionary psychology may be thinking, But a lady is simply not *built* for casual sex! In this anachronistic ladies-hail-from-Venus worldview, gentlemen desire to procreate prolifically while the women seek no more than a man to bring home the bacon. But this discounts such marvels of modern society as ladies who bring home their own bacon, citizens of Venus who screw each other's brains out, single gentlemen who are exceedingly troubled by the notion of fatherhood (forsooth, most of them), myriad birth-control options, and online personals. Besides, someone must be sleeping with all those lucky bastards— beg pardon, *cads*—and "crazy" Tracy from accounting only has so many nights in a week. Pluck be a lady tonight, after all.

While we report this table-turning with glee, it would be ignorant to assume it negates the need for manners. Now that it is held by many that even the prudent and modest maiden may enjoy sex for sex's sake, rules are even more important. They serve not to protect a lady's reputation (*so* last century), but rather to ensure that every deserving citizen— gentle readers, permit us a moment of vulgarity—gets fucked without getting fucked over. Gentlemen and ladies alike deserve their casual sex served with manners.

Protect Locally, Screw Globally

The gentleman or lady who neglects protection when dallying in casual sex does not deserve so much as a casual peck on the cheek. To ignore the threat to one's genitals is a gaucherie no shyness can excuse. Many ladies and gentlemen will forgo the awkward conversation and simply wrap up well—during one-time encounters in particular, this custom is too universally established for a protest against it to be of much avail. No one, however, can defend the practice as altogether *watertight*, as it were: A prophylactic will not protect your family jewels against all calamities (for more details, see p. 195). To be sure, dress-down sex means dressing up one's pride and joy. The conversation is of especial importance in the absence of a relationship, where there is no place for the (frequently erroneous) assumption "They care about me so I can trust them with my genitals." Simply lay it on the table (no, not *that*, vulgarian, the *topic*)—if your cohort is a lady or gentleman of substance, they will appreciate your candor. If they are offended by the conversation, then chances are they are not suited for the kind of laissez-faire loving you are after.

ONE-NIGHT STANDS

Creatures of the night, heed this: Etiquette is never more at home than when governing sex between two strangers who will probably never lay eyes (among other body parts) on each other again. In the one-night stand, there is no relationship to govern the interaction, and so we are forced to rely on the kindness of strangers. Only barbarians hold that manners are unnecessary if the first impression is also the last. For if today we are rude to our one-night stands, tomorrow we will stop holding elevators for strangers in a hurry, and by week's end we will be answering our cell phones in church. The following code of conduct should be observed by all ladies and gentlemen who indulge in one-time-only sexual liaisons. The more widespread these customs become, the more we can all enjoy what we crave without misgivings nor misconceptions:

- A gentleman or lady always lays their cards on the table before the strip poker begins. It is imperative you confirm that your date for the evening has no delusions of grandeur about a future together. There are still lovers who walk among us unfit for casual sex—they rely on the intimate embrace to show you how much they care, or to convince themselves that *you* care. The responsible cad or cadette weeds these persons out of the mix by being up front about his or her intentions.

- That said, it is uncouth to beat off a dead horse. Let us say the conversation is stimulating and the sex even more so. Let us say your bedmate suggests doing it again sometime as they head for the door. It would be unseemly to begin hyperventilating and gasp, between breaths, "I . . . am . . . not . . . looking . . . for . . . a relationship," as if you had just completed a marathon and they had suggested a brisk walk in the country to blow away the cobwebs. Perhaps they would simply like to be your booty call (see p. 82).

- To invite a new friend back to one's house and then seem to find their presence unwelcome is only a degree less cruel than inviting an acne-ridden dork to your lunch table in order to poke fun of his dress sense. It is not necessary to actually like your one-night stand, but it is polite to act as if you did.
- Conversation should be kept light and airy; it is expected that the subjects of life goals and family dysfunction will be avoided.
- Lovers would do well to remember that a thick, foreign accent is a delightful accessory to a one-night stand. In particular, persons whose native language is of the Romantic variety make ideal partners. It is uncouth, however, to fake a foreign accent in order to get laid.
- It is perfectly acceptable to use the encounter to experiment with acts that you consider out of character. After all, your partner will not think it is out of character—why, you have only just met! Ladies and gentlemen who fail to talk a little dirtier or get it on a little kinkier are missing out on half the fun.
- Because this act is not the beginning of a beautiful relationship, it would be inappropriate to rely too heavily on niceties such as lovey-dovey eye contact and mushy make-out session, lest your partner in crime get the wrong idea. Hard-core butt pirating is infinitely more apropos.
- A gentleman or lady is always discreet. Just because this person is a complete stranger to you does not guarantee they are a stranger to everyone in your social circle. (You would do well to log on to Friendster.com if you doubt the veracity of this statement.) Thusly, if you must brag, avoid mentioning their name or any distinguishing birthmarks (assuming, of course, that you exchanged names).

A Few Words on Departing

We know of a gentleman who took a new ladyfriend home one New Year's Eve. The connection was immediate, the ensuing flirtation deliberate, the innuendoes kinky, the sex kinkier. They kissed sloppily, fumbled with zippers, mussed up each other's hair. It was a perfectly debauched interlude. But in the thirty seconds between rolling over and passing out, this gentleman experienced that panic attack so familiar to persons not versed in the etiquette of the one-night stand: What will she expect of me in the morning? When he awoke to a hangover and the sun streaming in around nine, this gentleman reluctantly opened one eye to check on his bedmate. But she had vanished. The only sign he had even entertained company the previous evening was the slightly ajar front door. "I felt so used," he is fond of saying—not entirely ruefully—when he tells this story at dinner parties. "I suppose I would have appreciated a note, but her leave-taking did have a certain dramatic flair." Gentle readers, once may be a good story, but twice could deliver a serious ego blow, so we cannot in good faith allow you to sneak out merely to spice up dinner-party chatter the world over. When a fling fails to linger for the free, morning coffee, it leaves the

Mourning Sex

Whether or not casual sex is an appropriate salve for grief is a personal decision (and one of ethics rather than etiquette). But it is not vulgar to partake of grieving sex with someone who has made that decision—if you are satisfied they reached that conclusion while of sound mind, relatively speaking. It is a breach of etiquette, however, to assume an excessively charitable or pitying attitude when taking home (or accompanying home) a gentleman or lady in mourning. Once sex has been agreed upon implicitly, it is rude to delay the "healing," as it were, with constant questions as to the mourner's assuredness or state of mind. Besides, were they seeking solace in conversation, they would have called upon a friend or therapist. Instead, accept the fact that they are seeking solace in sex, and you are simply a vessel. It should be abundantly clear that this kind of one-night stand is not for the faint of heart—the one in mourning is permitted to take liberties with the usual rules of conduct, and their companion is not to complain. Additionally, the mourner determines the cuddle factor of a triste tryst—if they wish to spoon all night, it is elegant to bridle your claustrophobia and allow them to curl into you. Finally, let it be said, and emphatically, that if you do spend the duration of the night together, none but the churlish would depart without waking their melancholy flower—in this situation, a note will not suffice.

impression that the previous night's performance was sub par, or that they had buyer's regret. Therefore, the well-mannered lady or gentleman always makes a graceful exit from a one-night stand.

Once the sun has come up on casual sex, some form of acknowledgment of the previous night's dalliances is required. Prudence does not demand that you go out to brunch with the Sunday *Times* crossword—in fact, that is more intimacy than most one-night stands can support. On the other hand, leaving without saying a word makes a grander deal of the situation than is needed. A brief interlude of friendly banter and a self-deprecating joke for good measure is ideal. But if you simply cannot bear to wake the coyote who snores next to you, it is elegant to convey all this in a saucy note (sans phone number) left on the fridge or the dresser. The pillow would be cliché, not to mention suggestive of romance.

It is unbecoming to abuse the home-team advantage: While you may make a stealth exit from your partner's bed so long as you leave a note, you may never request, during the denouement, that your partner vacate your pad before daylight. And a gentleman or lady always offers their guest a cup of coffee or tea before showing them out.

However, dear readers—at the risk of being the bearers of bad news—you are not perfect. The time may come when you erroneously take your leave without a word. We do not condone such behavior, though we can offer an emergency etiquette guide, should you have a chance encounter with this person at a later date. (But remember, ladies and gentlemen, this is not to be relied on as routine.) There are a number of ways to approach a former one-night stand—mix and match any of the following as you see fit:

The Ice-Breaker: "Excuse me, don't I know you?"

The Inquisitive: "Hey, how's it going? Had any good one-night stands lately?"

The Small, White, and Therefore Evil Lie: "I tried to wake you, but you were in your REM cycle and couldn't be roused." (Not officially condoned by this book.)

The Big, Fat, Obvious and Therefore Funny Lie: "Sorry, I had to get home to wash my hair."

The Better Late Than Never: "I forgot to leave this with you the other day." (At which point you pass a note that includes above-mentioned witty banter and self-deprecating joke—to be sure, it is a tad involved, but it could work if jotted down quickly on a cocktail napkin after bumping into this person at a cocktail lounge.)

The T.M.I.: "I started to get the beer shits and didn't want to taint your bathroom." (Sure to guarantee the platonic nature of your relationship for all eternity.)

The Projection: "I can't believe you left without saying good-bye." The Here Are My Manners (our personal favorite, and your personal best): "Sorry I left without saying good-bye. That was terribly rude of me. Let me make it up to you and buy you a drink. And fear not, I will refrain from getting you drunk this time."

BOOTY CALLS

As gentlemen and ladies seasoned in the one-night stand are already aware, casual sex with a complete stranger is rarely good, clean, sporting fun. Either one party fakes nonchalance, or the other falsely claims serious intentions. Until this book becomes required reading in high school along with *To Kill a Mockingbird* (two ladies can dream), one-night stands are guaranteed to be occasionally messy and complicated. And if you leave behind your timepiece on their bedside table, as likely as not it will be on eBay by day's end.

However, the pull of one's sex drive and the desire for the regularity, comfort level, and sexual growth of congress with one person ought not to induce you to embark upon or linger in unhealthy romantic affairs. Behold, the booty call. Nothing better shows the standing of ladies and gentlemen, or their familiarity with the best usages of etiquette, than their ability to conduct a booty call with decorum. At its best, a fuck friendship blends casual intimacy with raucous, frighten-the-horses sex.

 **boot·y call—\bü-tē\ \'kȯl\, *n.* 1. A familiar acquaintance you may call on for booty (mutuality usually implied). 2. A call made to arrange booty with a familiar acquaintance. *Cf.* Fuck buddy.**

Perhaps due to the strong correlation between inebriation and off-the-books salacity, we are frequently lazy, sloppy, and thoughtless in our pursuit of a bit on the side. Many of us call exclusively upon exes, and thus the encounters are casual only as a result of attrition—where a protracted break-up—make-up cycle has served as so much paint stripper on a once emotion-drenched relationship, till all that is left is the screwing. Refined ladies and gentlemen do not limit themselves to their exes—the most elegant citizens know that even though *they* may eschew emotion when screwing old flames, it may not be (and probably is not) mutual.

Successfully navigating a booty call requires separating sex from all its attending emotions—not just love and the mushy stuff, but the jealousy, possessiveness, neediness, and shame that can accompany sex between friends (at least, more so than with strangers). It is the sublime understanding that fusing scent, touch, and body fluids can occasionally be just a phone call away and unencumbered by the formalities of movies, walks in the park, and candlelit dinners. It is mature ladies and gentlemen rutting as if they were seventeen again.

Let us take a look back at history. Well-educated citizens will know that the booty call is not new: Fuck buddies have been around for as long as people have been fucking their buddies. Which is to say, at least since the industrial revolution, when machines gave humans leisure time. But modern lovers recognize that there is now a new breed of booty call out there, as uncluttered as Erica Jong's zipless fuck but so much friendlier. It is infinitely less messy and misanthropic than booty calls of old. Ladies and gentlemen, we speak of appointment fucking. There is something in it for everyone with thirty minutes to while away and no long-term partner to while it away with: Ladies enjoy the sexual comfort level and more accessible orgasms that come with a lover who knows her body, and gentlemen simply enjoy the unimpeded and uncluttered access to sex. Well-bred ladies and gentlemen who approach no-catch nookie with tact and affability will find themselves in mutually arranged setups, frequently for months at a time. They are organized, even occasionally sober, about their casual sex. Most important, they get it on a regular basis.

Although we may be advanced sexual beings, for most of us, the only rule of booty calls is, You do not talk of the booty call. In fact, it is almost taken for granted. We still rely on a tacit understanding when it comes to casual sex with our friends and neighbors, and especially with our exes. But though we are loathe to admit it, we *do* talk about booty calls (with platonic friends) and we *do* have rules (we simply neglect to express them). It is ignorant to assume that a booty call is black and white and that everyone shares our own personal set of guidelines. The implicit, unlegislated booty call is a complicated procedure, due to varying agendas, the likelihood of miscommunication, and the chance of emotional intimacy. Gentlemen and ladies know that without rules, there are expectations, and those, by definition, make things messy. Even if you suppose you are without expectations, that in itself is an expectation: *That you not expect anything of me, that you not sleep over, that you not get mad if I don't call you back.* No longer is it permissible to follow this curious old-fashioned custom. It is time to manage those expectations with a set of rules for the modern booty caller.

Whom You May Booty Call

→ It is necessary to be attracted to each other, but it is not *de rigueur* to have anything else in common. It is simply a mutual desire to fuck one another's brains out when the need arises, whether that need arises out of low-grade depression, a taste for the sauce, or mere libido. The ability and/or desire to converse with each other is only necessary if one party requires that as foreplay.

- Both parties must be either single or in open relationships. In addition, ladies and gentlemen may find that complications and mixed messages are easier to avoid if both parties very recently exited long-term relationships.

- An ex one is currently friends with makes an ideal booty-call partner. An ex who has broken one's heart is not recommended, though a few (maximum three) booty calls may help provide closure—anything more must be considered an unsubtle and pathetic attempt to rekindle a relationship. An ex whose heart one has broken is off-limits, at least for twenty-four months. Do not emulate a vulgar lady of our acquaintance who, when she felt that a traditional booty call was improper in some fashion—perchance the ex had told her, "You have ruined my life, wench, now please leave"—would dial and hang up after one ring, knowing he would see the missed call and dial back. Making a vulnerable ex an accomplice does not let you off the hook, as it were.

- It is not required to seek out inner beauty. Rather, qualified booty-call partners include single, winsome bartenders (gratis alcohol, plus, they clock off just in time to receive your call) and ladies and gentlemen with "prominent assets." The booty call is carte blanche to be (or do) a sexual caricature.

When to Make the Call

- The gentleman or lady never makes a booty call more than a day in advance. An hour or two is considered foreplay, any longer and something better might present itself. A booty call is meant to scratch a fairly immediate itch.

➤➤ Unless otherwise agreed upon, after midnight on a school night is too late to call. On weekends, all calls should be made at least five minutes before closing time.

➤➤ If you do not desire an overnight guest, it is elegant to make the booty call before sundown. After sundown, we must recommend that you resign yourself to the possibility of entertaining all night long—unless you have express rules to the contrary, it is the only polite thing to do.

How to Make the Call

➤➤ It is prudent to treat one's booty-call contact information like that of one's dealer: Stored in a cell phone but never memorized, in case one wishes at some point to delete it permanently. Some elegant ladies and gentlemen prefer to rely on locations instead of digits, choosing a certain local spot where merely showing up after a certain hour is an indicator that one is in the mood.

➤➤ Upon misplacing a cell phone, the gentleman or lady always considers it a sign that it is time to trade players or retire.

➤➤ Booty calls are best made via caller ID–friendly devices. That way, the receiver can decide whether or not to take the call. If the receiver is not prepared to say yes, he or she should not pick up lest the answer offend or embarrass the caller. It is best to avoid the catastrophe that befell a gentleman of our acquaintance who turned down his booty call in favor of a late-night England vs. Argentina world cup soccer match. Though the lady was comfortable with the other women in his playing field, she took grave offense at placing second to soccer.

➤➤ If both cell phones are compatible, text messaging is the most civilized means of scheduling appointment sex.

➤➤ Though most booty calls are made after-hours, modern lovers would do well to remember that calls may also be made sober and in daylight.

➤ The considerate booty caller never gives out or dials a home number, especially if he or she deals in multiple partners. However, in the absence of mobile technology, the active booty caller who is playing a home game should keep the answering-machine volume turned to low.

➤ Booty callers should alternate who calls whom so that mutual interest is constantly re-established. If you have been the initiator more than three times without reciprocation, it is elegant to assume your friend has moved on. And if you wish to move on, it is acceptable to simply stop calling (or stop picking up)—especially if it was not a monogamous setup. (See the golden rule, in Addenda on p. 90, for notable exceptions.)

How Often to Make the Call

➤ You should not draw on one booty source more than once a week. Two weeks between appointments is ideal. Any more often and you risk drifting into a common-law relationship.

How to Conduct Yourself During an Appointment

➤ It is acceptable to be tipsy, but if you find yourself stumbling drunk and unable to perform the duties of the booty call, it is gauche to make that call in the first place. If the room is spinning, the gentleman or lady always goes home instead and passes out while attempting to masturbate. It is unspeakably rude to call if there is any chance you may vomit, or even dry heave, upon your fuck buddy.

➤ Both parties should be armed with prophylactics at all times.

➤ No matter how long you have been seeing your booty call, it is un-couth to intentionally leave personal items behind.

➤ A strict reliance upon the missionary position and the missionary position alone betrays a lack of sexual creativity that should not be tolerated among booty calls. Strike that pose sparingly.

➤ Few are aware of the influence upon morals exerted by that filthy habit of faking. The affected orgasm belongs in dysfunctional re-lationships and miserable one-night stands only. In the modern booty call, everyone gets at least one real one, whether delivered by oneself, the second party, or both parties.

➤ If you are not amused by the booty call, you are missing the point. They can be even more droll when both parties are sloshed, your wit drooping around the edges. Gentlemen and ladies always re-member that being funny is 50 percent what booty calls are good for. Having fun constitutes the remainder.

How to Conduct Yourself Between Appointments

➤ It is unmannerly to call your fuck buddy just to say "hi" (un-less you were friends for more than six months before you started swapping favors). It is correct to save the niceties for email.

➤ It is good manners to let the sun set at least once between ap-pointments with different buddies. If conflicting schedules pre-vent this, it is at least required that you shower before the second interlude.

➤ If your booty call is in your social circle and you are out together in a group, it is generally assumed—not to mention mannerly—that you will either go home together, or go home alone.

➤ Discretion is the better part of a valorous hookup: Just because it is a casual encounter, do not assume it is meant for casual con-versation. Do not lie, but do not brag either—it is unbecoming.

How to Discuss the Situation

➤ It is indecorous to refer to it as a booty call before the situation has been consummated.

➤ The gentleman or lady always ascertains whether they are in a monogamous booty-call situation. Some persons prefer to be the sole buddy their buddy is fucking, while others find plurality preferable (or at least tolerable). If nothing is discussed, one should assume plurality.

➤ One should avoid asking oneself, "What would my mother think of this arrangement?" And one should definitely avoid asking one's mother, "Mom, what do you think of this arrangement?"

➤ Well-bred citizens would not deign to think that six months of booty-calling each other connotes progression. Duration never implies acceleration, change, or growth—it is simply the same dirty thing happening over and over. Gentlemen and ladies know that a booty call matures into a bona fide relationship about as often as FOX's 11 P.M. headlining news item is truly newsworthy.

➤ If both parties know it is just the same dirty thing over and over, it is the height of vulgarity to make that point every time you do it. High-fiving your fuck friend and calling out, "Thanks for the casual sex, buddy" on your way out is inelegant. And repeatedly asking, "Are you sure you are okay with this?" or worse, "You do understand we're not together, right?" is condescending and insolent, not to mention self-aggrandizing. Such idiotic remarks and egoistic emendations evince a conceited coxcomb who has an inflated sense of their own "hand" in the situation.

➤ It is boorish to self-righteously refuse to avoid insulting others. One must be honest when a question is asked (about where this is going, about other booty-call partners one is seeing, et cetera), but unsolicited details should remain close to the chest. That said, omissions of details that would constitute a lie of omission should not be indulged in.

↞ The booty call does not mean "nothing." It simply means something different.

Addenda

↞ The above rules may be amended at any time if both parties are in explicit agreeance.

↞ The golden rule of booty calling is this: If you feel compunction, your instinct should be trusted. Few of us can completely separate sex from emotion, even if that emotion is not love (or something like it). No matter how casual the setup, it is correct to remember that your booty buddy is still a lady or gentleman, and not a fucking machine. If you are unable to play well with others, then we strongly advise you to invest in a good sex toy and stop tearing up the playing field for the civilized among us. This final rule may not be amended and trumps all others at all times.

When Your Booty Call Wants to Spoon

All booty calls are not created equal. There are gentlemen and ladies among us who are in the habit of adding elements of "dating" to the booty mix. Casual sex is no longer their sole goal; casual intimacy has now come into (the) play. We term this pattern of behavior The Free Trial. It is like this: Some ladies and gentlemen can sample the fudge outside Ye Olde Fudge Shoppe and keep walking, while others are indefatigably drawn inside to purchase five pounds of the macadamia nut—swirl. And so it is with relationships: Some ladies and gentleman can tolerate the occasional relationship sampler, though they do not desire an entire box of commitment—at least, not at this juncture. You may tempt them with free trials till the cows come home, but that might be just enough to keep them sated. It would be ignorant, however, to think that cutting off the supply would change their behavior: Some creatures simply do not need such sweetness in their lives the way others do. Especially when there is "fro-yo" to be enjoyed next door and "salt water taffy" to be found across the street. As a gentleman once said, life is like a box of chocolates. These Whitman's Samplers realize that a little closeness usually leads to hotter sex and more stimulating conversation over breakfast. Additionally, even the commitment-phobic are apt to enjoy the occasional cuddle or spoon—especially the gentlemen in their thirties and forties who find they are no longer at the ready three times in an evening.

Casual intimacy such as this might be termed a facsimile relationship. It is favored by gentlemen and ladies who have learned to appreciate the trappings of monogamy, such as home cooking and regular oral sex, but are loathe to be monogamous in those activities. However, lovers would do well to remember that this ticklish scenario requires an advanced degree in sexual etiquette. To enjoy casual sex, it is necessary simply to appreciate that sometimes sex is serious and sometimes it is not. But to appreciate casual intimacy, it is necessary to be casual about relationships, casual about people's expectations, and sometimes even casual about people's feelings. Neither dating nor casual sex exact so great a sacrifice as this, and thusly, we can neither condone nor legislate the behavior.

You shall know the Free Trial Citizens by the trail of broken hearts they leave behind, by the ease and aloofness with which they perform PDA, by the days and days they can go without needing to see your face or bury their face in your genitals—and you shall avoid them like scurvy. Unless, of course, you're a Free Trial Citizen.

All Good Things Must Come to an End

No matter how accomplished and mannered the gentleman and lady, at some point the same dirty thing over and over will become either depressing and/or boring. If you reside in the same zip code and see each other every few weeks or more, you should not expect the booty call setup to last more than six months. Time creates its own bonds—it would be uncouth to attempt to extend it any longer, lest you find yourself in another dysfunctional relationship. If, however, you live several states apart, the setup may be sustainable for years.

We know of a lady who was so pleased with her booty call setup that she pushed it into month seven. Then one night she encountered the gentleman at a party. He was with a lady who had a semi-permanent air about her, as evidenced by the coy tone of his introduction, her casual mention of his parents during a group conversation, the fact that they were out together before ten. She expected a pang of jealousy—it is always regrettable when one's booty call partner is taken off the market— but felt not a thing. She had so successfully cordoned off sex that she had temporarily suppressed her jealousy gene—and it was the least sexy feeling she had ever known. They never spoke again.

And so it is with booty calls, their beginnings and ends are usually arbitrary. It is what makes them work. It is what makes them need rules. It is what keeps them from breaking your heart. A nice place to visit, to be sure, but you would do well not to love there.

GROUP SEX: THREEWAYS, ORGIES, AND SWINGING WITH STYLE

There are times when gentleman and ladies feel like a nut, and then there are the times when they feel like a whole crystal dish of salted cashews, almonds, walnuts, and pecans. In a perfect world, all refined citizens would abide by the group-sex rules of engagement as laid out below. But in this world, it is rare enough to find respect for sex etiquette in one-on-one encounters. On what basis do we dare to dream that creatures of the night will develop manners, elegance, and tact once they start making the beast with six (or more) legs? On the basis that every lady and gentleman who reads this book will pay it forward, as it were. You are to pass on the wisdom contained herein. Additionally, we dream because refined ladies and gentlemen know to actively seek out advice on the proper protocol for salacious encounters that deal in multiples. While we may deem ourselves accomplished daters and lovers, few among us would claim to be either elegant or expert when it comes to a party for three or more. Happily, etiquette for group sex (or even just a threeway) is decidedly less humbling. Forsooth, gentle readers, hear us out: The expectation of group sex is that it is unequivocally casual, purely physical—because an insignificant percentage of the population is interested in long-term polyamory—and thus the rules are easier to establish and abide by. You doubt us? Then read on.

Threeway Etiquette for Today's Lady and Gentleman

It is out of fashion to refer to the threeway as a ménage à trois. It is simply so seventies. And *French*. The threesome is a pleasantly soft-core means of experimenting with bisexuality, taboo-busting, and exhibitionism/voyeurism. You would be surprised (or perchance you would not) how many ladies and gentlemen are open to a little one-on-one-on-one action; they are merely waiting for someone to ask politely. Refined lovers should simply beware the three threeway unpleasantries: jealousy, insecurity, and interrupted orgasms.

Advice for All Players

➤ A gentleman or lady never attempts to coerce a friend or partner into a threeway. All three parties must be equally willing accomplices.

- A gentleman or lady puts out gentle threeway feelers by giving backrubs, lingering after parties, initiating flirty conversations with lines such as "Have you ever wanted to? . . ." or "I have a friend who . . . ," et cetera. Then one calmly gauges the interest level from there.

- When two people share another person, more orifices will undoubtedly be explored. A gentleman or lady always showers first.

- Greed is one of the seven deadly sins namely because it ruins a good threeway faster than one can say, "My turn again!" A gentleman or lady is a giver: If one thinks one is getting enough attention, then one is probably hogging the bed.

- Just because it is a threeway, a lady or gentleman does not skip the foreplay. Besides, foreplay is a great, group activity.

- A gentleman does not assume he will stick *it* in; a lady does not assume anyone's *it* must be stuck in. And a lady is most certainly not agreeing to double penetration—or as it is known in polite circles, DP—unless otherwise stated. Some of life's best threeways do not include intercourse.

- A gentleman or lady prepares to feel left out and does not take this personally; it happens in all threeways. Polite activities while one bides one's time include footrubs, toe-sucking, nipple attention, and changing the CD.

- A gentleman or lady never has a threeway with a coworker. It is infinitely more elegant to find team players through friends, clubs, parties, or the Nerve Personals.

- A gentleman or lady thinks thrice before having a threeway with a good friend. Fuck buddies, however, are fair game.

- Threeway spooning and a table-for-three at brunch the morning after will probably feel more awkward than the actual dirty deed. A gentleman or lady should consider this before sleeping over.

Advice for Couples

You would do well to heed the following if you wish to keep the green-eyed monster at bay.

- Never surprise your partner with a third; threeways are not appropriate birthday gifts. A couple must choose their pinch hitter together.
- A gentleman or lady *never* uses a threeway as an excuse to "get it on" with a certain hottie "without cheating."
- In a heterosexual couple, if the third is male, let the gentleman in the couple lead the way; if the third is female, the lady in the couple leads.
- A gentleman or lady makes sure that his or her full-time partner gets a little more attention than the third.
- First-timers should probably stop short of intercourse (at least with the pinch hitter) in case the gentleman or lady freaks out the next morning. If no freak-out occurs, and all parties are partial to intercourse, then by all means fuck each other's brains out the next time.
- Post-coital chatter (after the third has departed) should include such heartfelt gems as "I couldn't wait to be alone with you"; "I couldn't stop thinking about you"; and "You're so much hotter."
- A gentleman or lady does *not* attempt to see the pinch hitter alone, unless it has been agreed upon with his or her partner in advance. Duels have been fought over smaller matters than this.
- Having a threeway to fix a broken relationship is as inconceivably obtuse as having a baby to fix a bad marriage.
- A gentleman or lady acknowledges the power of fantasy. Perhaps a pretend-threeway is more appropriate for one's relationship? At the very least, it is an agreeable means of testing the waters.
- The thrill of the chase can be a couples activity (fuck buddies may play this game, too). Seduce as a team: "Would you like to

come home with us?" works as well as any pickup line. The worst the potential third can say is no—at which point the couple goes home and fucks like bunnies anyway.

Advice for the Pinch Hitter

➣ The couple must ask first; a proper pinch hitter does not invite him or herself along.

➣ A proper pinch hitter never assumes he or she has sleepover privileges. However, if the couple invites you to breakfast, politely accept or decline as you see fit.

➣ A proper pinch hitter does *not* attempt to see one member of a couple alone, unless it has been agreed upon with his or her partner in advance. Otherwise, you can expect much more than merely a slap in the face with a pair of gloves.

➣ At the first sign of jealousy, prudence advises you to run—not walk—away.

➣ A proper pinch hitter accepts his or her permanent status as third runner-up. Just because the couple fucks each other does not mean you are going to get a turn.

Orgy Obligations

Consideration for the rights and feelings of others is not merely a rule for behavior in public, but the very foundation upon which successful orgies are built. Today's orgies—or "play parties" as they are known in the current vernacular—are more swings and roundabouts than swinging. It is commitment-free recreational sex at a cocktail party with a few (or a few dozen) cute friends, acquaintances, or near strangers. The play parties (at least, the ones that *you* would like to get invited to) are as removed from '70s key parties as *The Brady Bunch* is from *Sex and the City*. Forsooth, they are not for everyone. But they are for far *more* ladies and gentlemen than you might have thought. And they might just be for you.

How to Host a Sex Party

To be sure, there are times when a group make-out session will evolve naturally at the end of a pleasant evening spent with friends—one might blame it on the booze, the strip poker, or those "I Never" and "Truth or Dare" games. In fact, we would venture that if you have ever ended up playing late-night strip Trivial Pursuit with a group of friends and *nothing* happened, at least one person in that room had been hoping events would take a turn for the salacious. Oh, let us be candid here: *Everyone* had been hoping it would take a turn for the salacious. If you are uncomfortable in the role of gracious host, you might try throwing an impromptu after-party at your abode next time you find yourself out with a group of sexy young things. It is elegant to coax the mood with some evocative tunes. You would do well to play Scrabble for kisses, and then push the envelope—gently, discreetly—to see where things lead. You will find this most efficacious in a group of single friends, where all crushes (secret or overt) are fairly mild.

But why leave it to chance? The accomplished lady or gentleman knows how to throw together a charming afternoon of crumpets and tea. Should organizing an official sex party in order to guarantee a naughty outcome for all be so much more complicated or taxing? *Absolutment pas!* Below are a few things you should bear in mind before opening your door to the writhing masses. And remember, ladies and gentlemen: It is your party—you may come if you want to.

How Would You Like Your Orgy to Compare with Others?

Before attempting to host an orgy, it is advisable to assay someone else's play party, if possible. Appraise the competition to ascertain what helps the party flourish (perhaps Babywipes in every room for easy clean-up), what causes it to founder (perhaps Sting on the stereo), and what you should expect on your big night.

What Is Your Velvet-Rope Policy?

What if you threw a sex party and nobody came? It is prudent to invite a few instigators—ladies and gentlemen who will make out first, dance dirty first, get naked first, invite a guest to join them first. A less stilted time will be had by all if a few attendees are not orgy virgins. Other than that, your guest list is your prerogative. Do you desire an equal male/female ratio? Couples only? Singles only? Straighties only? No single men? All bi, all the time? Gay? Pad the numbers by requesting that every guest bring a few friends befitting an orgy. It would not be inappropriate to browse NervePersonals.com for "eager beavers," as we so fondly refer to them. It is acceptable to email out the invites, though paper is undeniably more tasteful (and impossible to "forward"). If friends of friends (or strangers) are on your guest list, it is perfectly couth to request an advance screening. After all, it would be unspeakably horrible to be forced to entertain guests who could kill a buzz from across the room.

Location, Location, Location?

For convenience and control, there is no place better than one's own abode. But perchance you have a nosy neighbor or landlord, maybe your modest lodgings cannot hold an event of this size, or perhaps you simply would find it unseemly to have guests fucking on your dinette. It is perfectly elegant to rent a space or book a hotel suite. It is advisable to ascertain in advance the likelihood of the party frightening the horses, especially if you will be providing props that could be misconstrued by intruders. ('Tis true, ladies and gentlemen have indeed been arrested for consensual participation at SM play parties.)

Will There Be Dutch Courage on Tap?

Orgy aficionados will tell you not to encourage daisy-chaining under the influence. Which leads yours truly to wonder, What *are* they thinking? Who *are* these people? Chances are, not all your guests will be such highly evolved creatures; stone-cold sober group fucking may be just a tad outside their comfort zone. After all, it was no mistake that the ancient Greek god Dionysus was the patron of both orgies and wine. A nice merlot or a hearty ale can make for a handy social lubricant. But the exacting host makes sure the guests know it is inelegant to get stewed: Keg stands do not put a soul in the mood. By the by, a buffet is unnecessary, though traditional sex parties (the ones your parents probably attended in the '70s) always seem to boast them. We fail to understand this curious habit. In fact, we find it rather unhygienic. The gracious host simply provides a stash of Power Bars for those who need to discreetly recharge.

What Is Good Orgy Feng Shui?

The gracious host puts some sexy CDs on shuffle so no one has to play DJ. It is recommended to play something without vocals. Advanced players have been known to select Peter Gabriel's *Passion*, though it is not uncommon for at least one guest to find group fucking to the *Last Temptation of Christ* soundtrack, shall we say, distasteful. The host should be particular to design a pleasing lighting scheme; it is odious and off-putting to catch sight of another guest's posterior pimples. It is polite to maintain a warm temperature so disrobing feels natural (or should we say, *more* natural). Scatter pillows everywhere and borrow extra mattresses from a friend. Vinyl sheets are practical, but have a hint of white trash about them. Better to request that all guests donate a set of clean sheets to the festivities. Or, if there is a trust fund from which you can draw funds, provide a plethora of soft, clean sheets for your guests. However you manage, you should expect that all surfaces being fucked on will become soiled. It is an oblation all hosts must simply accept and handle with aplomb. A bowl of condoms, dental dams, and latex gloves in every room is more than a nice touch: It is conscientious party planning. You might have some classy pornography playing in the background with the sound off for visual stimulation and inspiration. Take the phone off the hook, and ask your guests to turn off their cell phones.

Is There a Room with a View?

It is elegant to set aside one room or area as a sex-free (nudity optional) zone—your guests will appreciate the opportunity to regroup. In addition, every party has two guests who wish for nothing more than to huddle in the corner and discuss Kant's Categorical Imperative; orgies are no exception. Depending on how much space you have (and how fastiduous you are), you might want to demarcate areas for specific activities—undressing, mutual (mass) masturbation, couples-only spectator sex, ask-before-joining-in sex, jump-right-in-and-join-the-group sex, private hookups, etc. This approach will be more successful at larger gatherings, where there is the expectation of some organizing principles; if it is just you and five friends after a night at the bar, they might find it odd if you begin labeling the rooms.

When Is It Going to Get Interesting?

The perfect host knows how to get the guests in the mood. Sometimes scantily clad is sexier than totally nude—it is a tolerable idea to entreat your guests to wear their favorite underwear (though admittedly only a vulgarian would attend an orgy in their grandma's holey bloomers) and make it a lingerie party. You will find this cultivates an agreeable mood before the party hastens into good-grief-where-are-my-clothes territory. Other ways to turn your party spicy (besides serving sushi rolls with wasabi) include: Truth or Dare, strip poker, dirty dancing, footrubs, back rubs, body shots (rather trite, but invariably fruitful), Spin the Bottle (rather junior high, but invariably fruitful), Twister (you might even hap-

pen upon a new position), and feeding each other (perhaps that is the intent of the buffet). It is not intrusive to leave some instigating props lying around, such as massage oil, body glitter, lube, padded handcuffs,
blindfolds, and butt plugs. Perhaps even a Polaroid camera—a lens never
fails to arouse salacity, and there are no incriminating negatives.

What Are the House Rules?

Only the ill-mannered will look upon you as the prom chaperone if you set
a few rules. Guidelines help set expectations—and let guests know whether
they should leave the ball-gag at home. It is elegant to write them up in a
lighthearted email and send around after guests have RSVP-ed. Traditional swinging events encourage MF and FF action, but tend to frown
upon MM action (at least action of the genital kind). However, this kind
of antiquated thinking is terribly out of season. As the gracious host, you
must determine in advance what *you* wish to "encourage": Will you tolerate overnight guests? If not, it is polite to mention ahead of time when
last call will be announced. Kink or vanilla? BYO prophylactics? Cover
charge? (An entry fee is perfectly correct, especially if the host is renting
a space or providing the safer-sex supplies and liquor.) Is it "ask before
joining" or "jump right in"? No fake breasts admitted?

How to Behave As a Guest

There is no occasion when greater dignity of manner is required of both
ladies and gentlemen than the orgy. For a gentleman especially, no other
etiquette is so exacting. As a guest, abiding by the following rules will
ensure you are invited back; as a host, endorsing these rules will ensure
that the party goes off with a bang, or rather, *many* bangs.

- A gentleman or lady always showers before an orgy, and avoids
  overdosing on cologne. Guests who leave a trail of perfume in

their wake (be it body odor or Chanel No. 5) ought to be set among the predatory perfume promoters in the Bloomingdale's cosmetics department until they have learned their lesson.

- A gentleman or lady always dresses for the occasion. The sex is casual, the attire is not. A gentleman knows that flat-front pants are sexy, while pleated khakis are not.

- Statistically speaking, a gentleman or lady will be repulsed by at least one orgy attendant. One simply politely declines any advances made by said attendant, and attempts to mask the disdain. One avoids using the word "gross" and phrases such as "Not if we were the last two people at the last sex party on earth" and "I don't do charity work." One might try, "Thank you so much, but I'm all set right now."

- A gentleman or lady never takes a "no" personally. There is no accounting for taste.

- A gentleman always secures permission before delivering the money shot. The gentleman never performs a facial unless one is specifically requested.

- A gentleman or lady does not pressure anyone into being a joiner; some attendants may prefer to watch, or masturbate quietly in a corner.

- A gentleman or lady who chooses to watch understands that it is not like watching porn, that there is a difference between benevolent voyeurism and lecherous ogling, and that cheerleading is gauche.

- A gentleman or lady always asks before joining in (unless the house rules state otherwise). A gentleman especially understands that the two young ladies tonguing each other are not *necessarily* in need of his services.

- A gentleman or lady does not assume that nudity is an automatic open-invitation to a grope festival. Especially in the line for the powder room.

- A gentleman or lady is always discreet: Guests' identities are not to be revealed to anyone not in attendance.
- A gentleman or lady does not hog the hottie.
- A sense of humor complements the well-appointed orgy, but a gentleman or lady does not joke excessively or attempt to amuse fellow guests with such banal puns as "Come here often?"
- A gentleman or lady practices reciprocity and generosity of spirit and loin.
- A gentleman or lady *always* practices safer sex.
- A gentleman who is prone to "early arrival" rubs one out before leaving home.
- A gentleman or lady understands that while traditional swingers often applaud orgasms, other people find clapping weird.
- A gentleman who is simply there for the other ladies should keep this fact to himself. If a manly specimen brushes up against him, he does not freak out.
- A gentleman or lady avoids play parties that are: advertised in the classifieds, have a Star Trek theme, will involve coworkers, do not conduct prescreening interviews, have more rules than a mattress tag, have no rules, or are taking place at the Howard Johnson.
- A gentleman or lady always sends the host a thank-you note.

Swinging with Style

Distinguished couples who desire to screw their friends and neighbors—or "fuck the fences," as it is known in some, more relaxed circles—are advised to swing selectively. You would not be blamed for choosing to avoid free-love conferences where saggy, septuagenarian strangers can be found frolicking in sex-swing contraptions, eating potato chips, drinking Coors Lite, and banging the night away. The excruciating small talk, the one-eyed wonder worms assaulting your visage, the crumbs in your nooks and crannies . . . oh, the humanity!

No, it is far more elegant to take up with the Joneses. When one couple meets another and desires to get to know them *a lot* better—this is the kind of swinging we can really get behind and pat on the posterior. It is vulgar and outmoded to refer to this as "wife-swapping," though if it amuses the four of you to bandy about the term "spouse-swapping," that is tolerable (especially if neither of the couples is, in fact, legally married). The process from handshake to dickshake between two couples is not unlike courting: You make a connection, see each other for dinner and a movie, socialize more and more without ever really discussing it, all the while hoping the couple crush is mutual—and before you can say "Please pass the Stilton and walnuts" you find yourselves au naturel in a hot tub together. But if dating is an exacting procedure, then double-dating is doubly so.

The most elegant way to avoid complications is to set your boundaries ahead of time with your partner. These get-togethers frequently occur spontaneously and unexpectedly. Perchance the four of you shared two bottles of wine, finished the Blockbuster rental, and fortuitously stumbled upon some cable-access porn—then someone has the audacity to make an indecent proposal and, lo and behold, you are off to the races. Since it is impossible to read your partner's mind in this scenario, you would do well to initiate a conversation on boundaries and expectations sooner rather than later.

None but an ill-bred clown would attempt to coerce their partner into a swap. It is imperative that a husband and wife or boyfriend and girlfriend (or girlfriend and girlfriend, et cetera) be equally eager to get their feet wet in the swingers pool, and that one party is not dragging the other in for a dip less than fifteen minutes after dining. Additionally, a gentleman and lady always ensure they will be comfortable around the other swimmers. What if Mr. Jones's water noodle is more sizable? Is the gentleman capable of absorbing that, at least emotionally? The swinging couple needs to figure out ahead of time exactly what each partner will and will not do.

If it is your first time, it is perfectly polite to dawdle. Maybe you
swap partners for a PG-rated make-
out session before breaking and
heading to your respective abodes
for some old-fashioned sex with
your respective spouses. Or perhaps
one couple simply watches the other
get it on. Maybe you have sex with
your own partner while your neighbors do each other in the same bed.
Perhaps you find roving handwork
acceptable, but wish to proscribe
cross-couple oral or intercourse.
Maybe the ladies can do whatever
they wish in the middle of the bed so
long as the gentlemen stay on the
far side of their respective partners.
Or perhaps you are well-nigh ready

Four in a Bed

When engaging in a
fourway tryst, the well-
bred and amiable lover
will always put their
primary partner first.
This is of especial im-
port when swinging for
the first time; it would
be gauche to make any player feel ostra-
cized from the amorous struggles. Of
course, not all players need to be equally
entwined at all times—it is perfectly acceptable to masturbate on the side,
spectate, fetch the refreshments, et
cetera. But when in doubt, it is prudent to
give your spouse a little more attention
than the Joneses. At the very least, it is
polite to occasionally make meaningful
eye contact with your main squeeze while
touching another's naughty bits.

for *the* pièce de résistance of swinging: the literal spouse-swap.

However you define *the* double date, let us say the occasion of it
is upon you: The wine has been drunk, the porn is on, and you and your
partner have given each other the secret "fuck the fences" hand signal.
The first order of business is to ensure the other couple is of the same
mind. It is unnecessary to make them sign a contract, and it would
be uncouth to delineate the entire evening's game plan. Rather, a gentlemen and lady should casually suggest something they might find
enjoyable. At this point, if the other couple has not already had the
conversation about boundaries, it may be appropriate to retire the
topic and let them mull it over in private. There is much to be said
for delayed gratification, so save the salacious activities for another
night.

But perhaps the Joneses have been waiting for you to suggest this for six months and are ready to jump your respective bones, as it were. It is now pertinent to discuss a few specifics (safer sex, for one). But you would do well to remember that whatever you and your partner decide and whatever you agree upon with the Joneses, the evening will not progress the way you think it will or plan it to. Be advised that boundaries *will* get pushed. You may even experience twinges of jealously, envy, insecurity—especially if

> ### Mr. Jones and Me
>
>
>
> If the gentleman would rather not have Mr. Jones's tongue exploring his black hole, it is perfectly correct to say, "Perhaps we should keep our boxers on?" If you are concerned that your "good-touch/bad-touch" edict might stifle the merry mood, simply address the issues as they arise in the moment in your sexy boudoir voice. In addition, the elegant gentleman knows that "in the moment," certain acts (perhaps an impromptu sword fight?) are suddenly less unseemly—even, perchance, agreeable.

you are citizens of this planet. It is likely the liaison will not be as rousing as you dreamed, and it is more likely still that you will not be as elegant as you had hoped. It is therefore imperative to respect the rules of engagement the four of you agreed on, while remembering that civilized ladies and gentlemen know how to go with the flow.

Who Is That Sleeping in My Bed?

There are particular considerations for the gentleman and lady who desire to swap partners with another couple. The golden rule of manners as it pertains to this most traditional brand of swinging is that both couples must trust their partner and be secure in the relationship. It is the height of rudeness to engage another couple in any marital strife you may be going through, and it is ignorant to think that swinging can mend anything—it is simply a temporary distraction that will no doubt serve to make any problematic situation worse. In addition, it is odious and selfish to suggest swinging if you suspect you may have serious romantic feelings for the lady or gentleman in question.

Depending on the crossover friendships among the two couples, it may be appropriate for one lady to suggest a swinging time to the other lady, or for one gentleman to chat about it with the other over a game of squash—perhaps they have been intimate acquaintances since college. (However, the one broaching the subject should first garner permission from their partner.) The lady or gentleman receiving the salacious suggestion can then take the idea home to mull over with their partner. Or, if all parties are equally intimate, again, the subject may be raised in a group. It is generally considered inappropriate for one member of a couple to privately suggest the swap to the person of the second couple they would ultimately be fucking. For example, a heterosexual lady must never suggest swinging to her lady friend's husband, when neither her husband nor her lady friend are within earshot. No lady (or gentleman) should be so secretly familiar with another's lover.

Before the batons are passed, as it were, it is advisable to set a time when the four of you will reconvene—it would be most unpleasant for one of the temporary couples to be twiddling their thumbs in the living room while the other is currently engaged in round three in the guest room. Ideally, the temporary couples will each have their own bedroom. Or, if the four of you are away on vacation—the most civilized occasion for a virgin swing, in our opinion—then a hotel room each. During the swap, anything that reeks of romance should not be indulged in—pillow talk and meaningful eye contact is best kept to a minimum. If there is even the slightest chance you could fall in love with this lady or gentleman, then you should not be there. This is, however, the most civilized way to consummate and, in the process, quell the flames of a long-standing crush.

After the swap, you will be careful not to overshare with your primary partner. In fact, prudence advises you to determine in advance how much post-game analysis you each desire. Perhaps you both wish to go home, shower, spoon, and never speak of it again except in the vaguest of terms. Or maybe half the fun for you is dishing about your neighbors over espressos the next morning. Either way, be sure to dish with tact—no matter how breezy your partner seems, they are still human creatures with fluctuating emotions. If you have differing opinions on how much information is to be shared, the partner who desires the lesser amount of rehashing holds sway.

Denouement

Once all ladies and gentlemen have been sated, you will be faced with the age-old dilemma of casual sex: To sleep over or not to sleep over? If you are the kind of couple who requires wine to warm up to this kind of situation, you would do well to make a graceful exit before sunup; heaven forbid a perfectly pleasant fantasy night is marred by the cold, harsh light of day, a dual hangover, and your new best friends' morning breath. But if you take delight in that morning-after mix of awkwardness and intimacy (and if you care naught for what the neighbors think), then by all means stay the night and partake of brunch the next day. It is at this point you will most likely conclude that fourways are decidedly more civilized than threeways in any season, for no one need feel like a third wheel.

Whenever you take your leave, it is prudent to establish how much of the previous night's romp is fair fodder for the watercooler. It is perfectly acceptable to insist that what transpires at Swingers Club, stays at Swingers Club. This is a matter of privacy, not shame. It is only sensible to keep your tag-team talent off the agenda at the next country-club board meeting, lest *all* your friends and neighbors start knocking on your back door to knock on your back doors.

CHAPTER IV
Protocol for Specific Embraces

Just because a lady and gentleman are rutting like wild boars in heat does not mean they should forget their manners altogether. Politesse can coexist peacefully with raunch, and one may be twice the sick, dirty bastard *in* the bedroom if one is a nice, civilized person outside of it. Of course, not even the most modest among us desires to hear a deferential "May I please stimulate your clitoral hood, kind lady?" in the throes of passion, or a gracious "Thank you *ever* so much for the delightful oral pleasure" after it. Not unless we are engaging in a game of "I'm lady of the manor, you're the errand boy" (or "I'm lord of the manor, you're the chambermaid"). But lovers would do well to remember that there *is* nevertheless an elegant and an inelegant way to be an animal in the bedroom. The following guidelines should help you be the kind of beast that leaves bite marks your partner brags about over tea—rather than the kind that has "accidents" all over the new rug.

ORAL OPERATIONS

The golden rule of manners as it pertains to dining downtown is this: Consider it the equivalent of a gratis meal at a Jean-Georges establishment. It is a sheer delight simply to be there, and thus it is becoming to act as if that is so. A gentleman or lady should also bear in the mind the following:

→ When the best chefs in the country insist that there be no salt and pepper shakers on the tables, then their dishes do not require salt or pepper, and to request either would be an insult. A courteous diner eats everything exactly the way the host suggests they do, and exactly the way it is presented to them. The polite pleasurer never contradicts directions with comments such as, "But my ex used to *love* it when I did that," or "But I have been practicing that move all week!" or the unforgivably tactless, "Well! If this isn't the poorest I ever tasted!"

→ A gentleman or lady never expects their pleasurer to know exactly how he or she takes it. The refined receiver offers hints, always phrased in positives. Recommended nudges include "Right there oh my God yes" and "Please, sir, may I have some more?"

→ Of all things horrible, it is the limit to push someone down by the shoulders, using their ears as a steering wheel, or to accelerate the pace by pushing on their head as if it were a toilet plunger. These gaucheries are not considered "hints."

→ The decorous diner understands that a chef must eat, too. Oral pleasure is a reciprocal activity, and a gentleman or lady cannot expect to receive head any more often than he or she proffers it. A gentleman or lady *may* request oral pleasure without reciprocity on the following occasions: it is one's birthday (no half birthdays); one has been laid off; one's favorite team lost (major championship games only, no mid-season games); one's pet has died (in the case of a goldfish passing on, it is the pleasurer's call); one styled one's short-and-curlies in a manner pleasing to one's partner; one's partner lost the "guess how many pennies are in the jar for free oral sex" bet; one's partner fell asleep the last time one was going down on them.

→ A gentleman or lady does not find it grotesque to make out with their partner after receiving head. However, diners who are particularly sloppy eaters would do well to subtly wipe their mouth on the bedsheet or the back of their hand mid-ascent.

- A gentleman or lady keeps a clean "house" when expecting company. If the most recent wipe was not a clean one, a gentleman or lady always showers (especially if he or she favors the triple-padded, terribly soft, *clingy* brand of toilet paper). A gentleman or lady understands that pubic topiary is a matter of aesthetics, not hygiene (see p. 209).

- A gentleman or lady avoids ingesting substances that cause the taste or smell to be slightly "off" down there. Common culprits include asparagus, coke (not the trademarked kind), cigarettes, red meat, or coffee.

- The polite pleasurer makes occasional eye contact while giving head, but avoids engaging the receiver in stare downs. It is not bad manners to close your eyes while receiving if that helps you get to your happy place—especially for the ladies who may need a little help staying focused—though the refined receiver will occasionally take a peek to check in on their partner. A gentleman or lady knows that a mid-sesh wink, by either party, is extremely hard to pull off with grace.

- The refined receiver never says, "You look like you have a pube mustache, ha ha ha!" or "Yeah baby, walk like an Egyptian!"—or anything else implying one's partner looks anything other than exquisite down there.

- Just as it would be unseemly to make fake gagging noises if Jean-Georges served you escargots, so is it churlish to treat a stray short-and-curly as something odious. Simply remove it with your fingertips without any fuss or take a large gulp of water while maintaining a gracious visage. The polite pleasurer does not try to make light of the situation by flossing with said hair.

- A gentleman or lady never hums while giving head during the first two months of a relationship.

When you are snacking on a sausage and feel your gag reflex start to engage, it is not rude to disembark. Breathe deeply, drink some water, excuse yourself if need be—and worry not that your partner will object. After all, no one gags on an exceedingly teeny cocktail frank.

Notes for the Gentleman Receiver

❧ The average throat is approximately two to three inches deep; the average tumescent manly specimen is approximately five to six inches long. The gentleman receiver does not need a degree in physics to understand the ramifications of this. Ergo, no thrusting unless it is requested.

❧ The gentleman receiver understands that stamina is not generally appreciated in this arena. When it comes to blowjobs, there is no such thing as arriving fashionably late.

❧ The gentleman receiver always announces his impending arrival so that his pleasurer may decide whether to spit, swallow, or top him off with a bit of handwork. He never tells a lady (or another gentleman, for that matter) how to dispose of his seed. However, the sophisticated sucker will want to avoid roaming about an unfamiliar house with a mouthful of come in search of a bathroom or waste receptacle. (Assuming, of course, that the couple has already had that very civilized conversation about their respective sexual histories, see p. 194.)

❧ A gentleman never refers to a woman's behavior as "unladylike," for the gentleman does not want karma to curse him so that he is never the beneficiary of the best, most unladylike behavior: the blowjob.

The Mythical Sensual Benefits of the 69

A lady is never prettier than when she has a cock in her mouth, and the gentleman never looks so courtly as when he is giving head. And so, we ask, why the 69? The view is atrocious.

The most infamous of sexual embraces is a rite of passage, a notch in the belt of youthful experimentation. What lady or gentleman has *not* steamed up the windows of their parents' Volvo in this arrangement? Overexcited and overanxious, pressed for time and even more pressed for space, it is understandable that a teen may consider a spontaneous impression of the yin and the yang to be a good idea. A cultivated lady or gentleman knows otherwise.

Still, some inelegant citizens—namely porn stars, "kids at heart," and lovers who listen to smooth jazz—insist on propagating the mythic sensual benefits of the 69. The well-mannered lady or gentleman may politely correct them. It is acceptable to name renowned and annoying Tantric lovers like Sting as a disincentive, and to remind the vulgarian how often a 69 ends in frustration. Developing a rhythm in said stance requires the coordination of a Cirque du Soleil performer, the patience of a Buddhist monk, and the motor skills of a bonobo ape. To say nothing of the concentration skills required. A gentleman or lady will note that the horse attached to the buggy wears blinders, and the responsible citizen never talks on a cell phone while driving—it is because distractions cause accidents (and typically not the happy kind). At the very least, one's automatic bodily response inadvertently becomes an attack of the killer genitals on a loved one's face, making breathing tricky and choking a very real possibility. And once you lose your head in the heat of the moment, your dear friend may lose *their* head.

GEYSERS, FACIALS, AND PEARL NECKLACES

There comes a time in every gentleman's life when he desires to pull out and impersonate Old Faithful, just for the visual. Or perhaps there come *many* times. Ladies, too, may appreciate the visual—it is as pleasing a spectacle as the hickey (though hopefully not one that may be espied the next morning). The gentleman ejaculator avoids rushing the clean-up as if he were a misbehaving puppy who just peed in the parlor—he wipes his lover down tenderly and grace-fully, treating the act as part of the postcoital bonding. If he happens to make a particularly large deposit, he leads his partner by the hand to the shower so they may rinse off together.

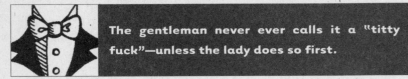

The gentleman never ever calls it a "titty fuck"—unless the lady does so first.

Facials, in particular, remain one of the foremost taboos—and taboo-banishing sex is often the most fervid, in that "so wrong it's right" man-ner. However, the well-bred gentleman knows that in some cases, it is *so* wrong that it is simply wrong. Performing an at-home facial without first garnering permission is one of those cases. Coming on a person's face is a loaded act, like slapping them in the face (which can also be a "nice touch" in the middle of sex, see sidebar on p. 144). Projectiles aimed at one's visage—a glass of water, a loogie, a cream pie, a fist—are rarely hallmarks of affection. They are more often thrown to insult and/or hu-miliate, usually when there is an appreciative audience. You will also no-tice that the above-the-neck money shot is a staple in porn—a genre in which ladies and gentlemen are rarely treated as such. In fact, its preva-lence in porn is another reason why people averse to cheesiness do not go gaga for the facial themselves. And let us not forget that a gentleman's juice stings like a mother if you get it in your eye.

To be sure, not all facials are created equal. Like dining on fish eggs, context is king. If you are a poor lout whose mother did not love him enough and consequently treat every lover who has the misfortune of crossing your genital path as if she (or he) were a side of beef, then the facial is a true act of degradation. But if you call your mother once a week, are in a mature relationship, and you *both* are tickled by it, then the facial is an act and nothing more—an agreeable form of role-playing. If you mark your territory because you believe your partner is your property, then you deserve to be evicted without notice. But if you mark the territory because you fancy the visual, then it is simply a way to make things merrier without waking the neighbors.

The following guidelines should help you butter your lover's head correctly. For the sake of ease and clarity, we shall assume the gentleman's lover is a lady.

- A gentleman never assumes a lady is doing him a favor, or that she will be swallowing (or is that *not* swallowing?) all her feminist pride to please him; plenty of ladies find it agreeable, too.
- Only the yahoo attempts to win over a lady by listing a facial's benefits to her complexion. Semen does indeed contain protein, which can have a *temporary* tightening effect on wrinkly skin . . . until the lady rinses off in the powder room. And semen does indeed contain lipids, amino acids, and prostaglandins that in other products have been shown to improve skin, but there is no concrete evidence that those ingredients in ejaculate have the same effect here. To suggest they do is beyond tacky.
- A gentleman who has never come anywhere but in the condom before might consider building up to the facial: stomach, breasts, back, neck (known as a "pearl necklace" in the vernacular). Or he

can simply ask his lady friend where she would like him to make his deposit.

- A gentleman knows that when it comes to safer sex, he should keep his snake in its latex skin if it is wriggling anywhere *near* Vagina Valley. He is also aware that ejaculate can spread disease if it comes into contact with *any* mucous membrane, not just the vagina (e.g., mouth, eyes, open cuts, the chocolate starfish).

- If a gentleman wishes to request a facial in advance, before entering the bedroom (so the sex is not imminent and the pressure is lifted), he avoids raising the subject at breakfast or during rush-hour traffic. Instead, he waits until the next time he is sharing a fine wine with his lady, when they are playing a little footsie and things are getting a tad frisky. At this point, he may lean in and say something like, "You're so sexy, you make me want to do dirty things. I'd really love to defile your face, if you receive my meaning." If a gentleman wishes to appear sexy, he should always check for red-wine teeth before leaning in.

- If a gentleman suddenly desires a facial in flagrante delicto, he should simply make the request part of the dirty talk: Everyone is more amenable to suggestion in the throes of ecstasy.

- A gentleman always bears in mind that for most ladies, ejaculate on the face becomes unsexy (not to mention chilly) exactly 5.3 seconds after the last orgasmic shudder. Ergo, he never requests a facial unless he has a box of Handy Wipes on the bedside table. If he has only Kleenex on hand, a true gentleman settles for a pearl necklace.

- Even the fastidious gentleman should not express displeasure if he gets some on himself, especially if the lady has yet to come. The genteel man appreciates the gravity of the fact that ejaculate is *on her face*.

- A gentleman knows that nothing says "the pretend defilement ends here" quite like a good cuddle.

When the Lady Is a Spurter

Gentle readers, you already know that anything gentlemen are capable of, ladies are too—except, perhaps, effectively utilizing a urinal. Ejaculating is no exception. Although, to be sure, while there are some women who are possessed of the ability to squirt across the room, others will themselves be exceptions to the ejaculation exception. (Ejaculation evangelists claim it is within all ladies' natural ability to squirt; they will tell you that some ladies simply squirt so little and with meager force that it is inconsequential.) Should you be so privileged to witness such a feminine spectacle in action, it would be utterly discourteous to *take* exception to it.

Female ejaculation is usually associated with provocation of the mystical G-spot. You will forgive us for dispelling the mysticism: The female urethra runs above and parallel to the vagina and is surrounded by spongy erectile tissue. During arousal, this sponge swells, and can be felt through the top wall of the vagina, about two inches in. Land-ho, ladies and gentleman, this is the female G-spot! Should you and your partner find yourself struck by G-wanderlust, it is advisable to remember the following points of etiquette:

- Both parties should be aware that the firm and steady stroking of the G-spot will be agreeable to some ladies—and entirely *disagreeable* to others. Some ladies will find it irksome, or even painful, others may simply be overwhelmed by the urge to pee. There is no reaction to G-spot stimulation that is abnormal, and to suggest so is rude.
- Even if the lady finds it agreeable, she may nevertheless experience the urge to urinate. Assuming she has already relieved herself, if she relaxes and goes with the flow, as it were, she may find she produces a flow of her own—anywhere from a few drops to a veritable waterfall of clear fluid will be expelled from her urethra.

The civilized gentleman or lady knows that the ejaculate is not urine. If he or she wishes to sniff the sheets to confirm this fact, it is polite to wait until one's guest has left the room. And even if the lady in question has a small bladder, and a bit of urine did escape her secondary lips when she was overcome with ecstasy, do not make a fuss, and certainly do not make her feel contrite for it.

➤ It is gauche to pressure a lady to perform in this manner, as if she were a circus animal. It is gauche in the extreme to invite comparison to one's ex-girlfriends or porn stars who *were* capable of performing in this manner. To do so is not, as the deluded gentleman may tell himself, "inspirational"—to do so is rather to suggest that she has been an unsuccessful lover.

➤ If a lady rains down on you, only a vulgarian would throw in a penny and make a wish.

BEING ANAL

It is only the uncivilized lady or gentleman who believes that backdoor friends are always a pain in the ass. In fact, when we hear otherwise enlightened ladies and gentleman categorically dismiss bum love—or just laugh it off—it makes us wonder what kind of Neanderthals have been knocking on their backdoors.

Unfortunately, anal exploration has not been linguistically blessed, as the modern gentleman or lady who wishes to discuss rear matters will have learned. Most of the slang that describes playing the B-side involves a variation on the color brown. It has been more than a century since Oscar Wilde saw fit to put buggery to paper and Rimbaud penned his "Sonnet to the Asshole," yet the act is still considered more punchline than storyline. Only *you* can change that.

Therefore, a gentleman or lady should frown upon anal giggles and avoid terms such as "Hershey highway," "dirt road," and "cornhole." More acceptable terms of endearment for the body part include "ass," "puck-ered kiss," "rose bud," and "starfish"; for the act itself, consider "back-door love," and the evergreen "anal sex." A merry gentleman or lady may refer to the act, in jest, as "using the servant's entrance"—though never in front of actual servants.

The second problem encountered by the anally inclined lady or gentleman is this: Discussing anal play means discussing matters of di-gestion and discomfort. How *inelegant*. But the modern citizen knows that these are trifling matters; the rumors of poo and pain have been un-forgivably exaggerated. The odious boors spreading them (the rumors, that is) have undoubtedly had bum sex incorrectly. Either that or they are the banes of anal who think there is only *one* proper way to have sex. The educated gentleman or lady should politely correct them.

The well-bred gentleman or lady knows that approaching the ass with aplomb is a simple matter of preparation, lubrication, and fiber in one's diet. It is unfortunate that these graces are not yet synonymous with ro-mance. Old-fashioned notions still prevail: that a gentleman or lady should not plan sex or discuss sex in advance, that sex education should not be part of a lady's trousseau, that a gentleman and lady should never require props like man-made lubricants or strap-on dildos, and that all the parts should fit together *just so* the very first time. It is not bad man-ners to suggest to your partner that you shop for sex toys, experiment with lube, or eat bran flakes for breakfast. If you can convey all that with decorum, you will be loving like the ancient Greek gentlemen in no time.

A gentleman *never* tricks his lady into anal sex by "accidentally" using the wrong entryway. This antiquated attempt denotes a cad who has learned his manners from vulgar publica-tions. Let there be no surprises—uninvited guests should be turned away at the door.

Tossing the Salad

A gentleman or lady knows that while the open-mouth kissing of dogs and cats is unseemly and absurd to many, the kissing of assholes is to be encouraged to all. First and foremost, you should procure (and actually use) a dental dam—it is the only way to truly ensure you will not receive or spread any unwanted parasites, bacteria, or viruses. It is additionally correct to shower immediately before requesting a rim job. A gentleman or lady never says, "Kiss my ass," unless in a consensual role-playing scenario with their partner (though a coy "Would you tell me a French joke?" is acceptable). In addition, the well-rimmed citizen will avoid the temptation to call their rimmer an "ass-kisser." A gentleman or lady knows that it gets lonely back there at the asshole, and therefore spoons with particular attention after the blessed event. No gentleman or lady should permit their partner to be so familiar with their asshole if they are feeling gassy. If the urge suddenly arises, he or she simply says, "My turn now" and switches places. Every gentleman and lady should try both "ends" of a rim job at least once in their lifetime. And the courteous receiver does not say, "That did nothing for me" after their partner has been kissing ass for twenty minutes. At least, not within the first twenty-four hours of a rim job.

Strapping One On with Style

The heterosexual gentleman ought to remember that the beauty of the asshole is precisely that it is the great equalizer. If the lady is agreeable to keeping her servant's entrance open, then the gentleman should leave his own back door ajar at least once. It is anachronistic and in excessively bad taste to refuse it on principle. In fact, many a pleasant mind fuck (as well as much exquisite prostate attention) has occurred as a result of the gentleman permitting his lady to strap one on.

A lady should be particular to move at a slow pace and always love with care, as one would hope the gentleman in question did with her own puckered kiss. If this is the gentleman's derriere debut, it would be ungracious (not to mention decidedly uncomfortable) to begin with a strap-on. She should start with some gentle pinky-finger poking. And the rear-quarters visitor should furnish herself with ample lubricant. A lady's saliva will not cut the mustard, so she should purchase a hardy, man-made lubricant for the occasion (we suggest the aptly named Probe). A man who is unduly hirsute may wish to trim his area hairs to allow for a smoother entry.

The Gentleman Spot

A cultivated gentleman is on a first-name basis with his prostate—that small, round gland so key in the production of semen, which can be felt about two inches up his bumhole (toward his navel). He may even refer to it as his own personal G-spot, especially after a particularly pleasurable session of backdoor loving. Only the ignorant gentleman would refuse anal attention because "it feels disagreeable when my doctor checks my prostate"—he knows that would be the equivalent of a lady renouncing sex after an unpleasant visit to the gynecologist.

When it comes to equipment, a lady may pick out her harness. However, the dildo is always gentleman's choice (though it is quite en règle, in these aesthetic times, for the lady to offer input on color and design). Proper equipment is imperative if a merry time is to be had by all. How many times has a dildo slipped out of an ill-fitting harness just to stay lodged in a gentleman's rear like an obscene turkey timer? One too many. To be sure, some modern citizens are possessed of stronger constitutions than others, but most will find technical difficulties unseemly and distracting. To avoid accidental turkey impersonations, lovers would do well to settle on a harness with an adjustable ring size—this will permit the couple to experiment with various dildo sizes while avoiding the dreaded "wobbly dick."

Though the masculine graces might suggest that a gentleman should "be a man" and choose a silicone specimen as large as his own, this is inadvisable. He should start slight and build up gradually. Butt plugs may look like more genteel backdoor friends, but they are designed to arrive and *stay* (as opposed to dildos, which are more active house guests). Gentlemen ought simply to choose a modest specimen specifically designed for the rear (long and curved rather than straight and stubby), with a flared base that fits the ring of the harness.

It is not the correct thing for a lady to approach her gentleman with such force as would frighten the horses. She should let him ease onto the dildo at his own pace, so he can guide her in at the most comfortable angle. No thoroughbred lady would ever get carried away and start thrusting like a steam-engine piston while yelling "Who's your daddy?" She may, however, yell "Who's your daddy?" if she can express this sentiment without jackhammering.

A mannered lady always exits in a calm and orderly fashion, even if the gentleman swears there is a fire in his cabin. And finally, it is a refined act of courtesy to give him a nice blowjob or a cuddle (again, gentleman's choice) and tell him he has been a very good—or perhaps a very bad—boy.

 ## SHARING TOYS

It is not too much to say that more toys in the bedroom would have saved many a relationship from ruin. The interchangeability of accessories makes for interesting variety. Sex toys have solaced many a lonely soul and enlivened many a leisure hour—not to mention many a leisure fuck. However, people of breeding and true refinement know that having *one* vibrator lying around for *every* flavor of the week is ill-mannered, and somewhat gross. Everyone deserves their own personal sex toy. Nothing says "you're one of many" like an old used vibe—no matter how long your butler spent buffing and polishing it.

That said, the modern lover should certainly be creatively attentive to their partners' possible prop needs. True courtesy dictates that you buy a new toy for every new guest you may be entertaining. To do otherwise would be flagrantly indecorous and your guests would probably resent it as the greatest insult. When introducing a new toy, one should broach the subject tactfully, delicately, and if the lady or gentleman seems game, one may present them with their new, unopened gift, as part of the foreplay. (Fancy wrapping with ribbon and a bow is an exquisite touch.) Later, after both parties have seen the face of God and are smoking their Nat Browns and exchanging dewy glances, we insist that you let your guest keep the gift. And no, you may not ask for it back if and when the relationship sours.

The one excepting clause is this:

Gifts

Lingerie, nightwear, or provocative clothing should never be bequeathed to a partner as an indirect gift to oneself. To bestow an ensemble of, say, leather and lace upon a person who is vegan or has taste is not only selfish, it is insulting. The thong given to a committed boxers man is an unwelcome burden; you back him into a corner with self-interest disguised as kindness, forcing him to swallow his pride in order to make *you* happy. Yet the sole concern of a gift should be the *receiver's* pleasure. This rule does not apply if you and your partner have discussed the "little number" in question first, or you have been together more than a year.

Many modern ladies require specific clitoral stimulation in order to get off, and may be accustomed to achieving this with a toy. It is therefore not impolite for her to suggest using her own toy, and the civilized gentleman should not take offense at the absence of packaging or at the size of the toy (in the case of twelve-inch, ten-pound, vibrating dongs). If, however, the gentleman is provoked to suggest, "Anything the vibe can do, I can do better," the lady should by all means take him up on the challenge.

SHARING PORN

The cultured couple knows that watching pornography is like working out—it is not *necessary* to do it together, but it cannot be too highly recommended as sweaty, heart-racing, flushed-cheeks foreplay. And just because the lady is a mud-wrestling connoisseur while the gentleman prefers yoga, does not mean they cannot enjoy the occasional stroll through the park together. The point is to think outside the (ahem) box when it comes to porn.

Let us consider the typical heterosexual couple. A gentleman who is having difficulty persuading a lady to share his pornography should consider whether his approach to the "screenings" is a little *manly*. He should take a close look at the male stars in the average gentleman's porno. He will notice that the men are not actually that handsome (after all, a gentleman watching porn does not wish to be distracted by feelings of inadequacy). Additionally, the gentleman should inspect the female stars from his lady-friend's perspective. He will find that these stars are mostly bottle blondes with bad fake tans and floatation devices for breasts—not most ladies' idea of feminine beauty. And the typical delivery-guy plot devices are gauche in the extreme to most ladies—no wonder she would rather be doing her taxes. The modern lady finds it a little hard to relate, or even just suspend her disbelief, when it comes to the typical bodies, plot, and dialogue of today's skin flicks.

Whether you are part of a hetero or a homo couple, it is imperative to select pornography together—to find titles that deliver you both to the gates of ecstasy. Or at least get you halfway there—because the modern relationship is built on compromise. The following guidelines for sharing porn should help you both cultivate a more compromising attitude (which one would hope would lead to more compromising positions, too):

- The gentleman or lady does not assume that sharing porn automatically means renting a video. Read an erotic novel aloud to each other, or listen to an erotic recording. (Ponytailed gentlemen may take more naturally to this suggestion.)
- Because the majority of pornography is not made with the ladies in mind, the lady always has final say in the video store.

◄► Where possible, a gentleman or lady avoids renting a title he or she recently shared with a previous partner. If three or more years have passed since the viewing with said ex, a title is once again fair game.

◄► A gentleman or lady always steers clear of titles featuring exes or family members. Titles featuring former teachers or babysitters, however, are recommended.

◄► A gentleman or lady never "surprises" a partner with a niche fetish title in the first six months of a relationship.

◄► Things not to say while watching porn with one's partner: "Wow, I didn't know they came that big!"; "How come you never spurt that far?"; "Oh! I remember doing that with my ex!"; "See? She doesn't have any pubic hair."; "Mom?"

◄► A gentleman or lady knows that even the patriotic porn enthusiast does not always insist on buying American. Foreign is agreeable; foreign without subtitles even more so.

◄► While there should be no expectation of sex after a shared porn viewing (and there should certainly be no expectation of a specific sexual act), a gentleman or lady never rushes straight off to the supermarket/office/pizza parlor.

◄► If the film gets one of you in the mood and makes the other swear off sex for three months, the horny lady or gentleman may rub one out. In fact, the horny lady or gentleman in a relationship may *always* rub one out unless the two of you are running late for dinner or your partner needs help assembling furniture.

◄► A gentleman or lady does not nag their partner to relinquish their college porn, nor does he or she attempt to force their partner to share their college porn.

◄► A gentleman or lady does not store porn magazines on a coffee table, in a magazine rack, or in the bathroom.

◄► When perusing the selection at the video store, the cultured couple avoids box covers displaying animals, babies, or U.S. flags.

THE FASTIDUOUS FETISHIST

In polite society, it is often said, good taste never touches extremes. But in the bedroom, it is not considered imprudent to explore extremes. You ought to remember that good manners in the bedroom means reserving all judgments. When hearing of a partner's fetish for the first time, it is not the correct thing to listen with one's head tilted to the side as though one were Barbara Walters or a Freudian therapist. Nor should you make a parade of your limited knowledge of their longtime hobby ("Oh, I saw a website about that the other day!"). Simply listen with an open mind, and if the conversation excites curiosity, let the frolicking begin. If the conversation excites disgust, it is a breach of etiquette to suggest one's partner is a freak. Rather, emphasize your *own* discomfort with this particular sport. You should certainly not feel pressed to partake, and your partner should not apply such pressure. Even the most modern of ladies and gentlemen are entitled to find some things dirty in a good way, others dirty in a bad way, and still others just plain dirty.

When *sharing* a fetish with a partner, one should never apologize—it is unbecoming to express regret for one's turn-ons, assuming they are legal. And do not assume anything about how your partner will take the naughty news: The most pierced, tattooed, sexually aggressive woman in the diviest dive bar in town might have a particular fondness for the missionary position, while the lady in pearls might like to be peed upon. There is no way to ascertain in advance who falls where on the gross-out (or freak-out) scale. Prudence advises you not to raise the subject on the first few dates—unless it comes up naturally, in which case one is obliged to tell the truth. However, one may garner hints as to someone's sexual progressiveness. It is advisable to wait until the conversation takes a turn for the lascivious—as it is wont to do eventually. At this point, a gentleman or lady is permitted to ask of their date, "What is the craziest thing you have ever done in bed—or been asked to do?" If your date responds, "I once did it standing up," you may consider this a sign that he or she is a touch too timid for the likes of you.

However, the only way to truly verify a response is to raise the subject delicately but specifically. The fastidious fetishist explains that this is a very intimate act for them, that it is their favorite taboo to contravene. It is correct to use confident language that makes the act sound sexy rather than dirty-old-man-in-a-raincoat vulgar. A gentleman or lady avoids saying, "There is this uncanny thing about me that I am obliged to explain to you," and instead begins, "It would be so intoxicating if you would do me the honor of . . ." Do not neglect to reassure your date that some of the best sex makes one feel sullied—both inside and out.

Many accomplishments are necessary for the enjoyment of a fetish, but it begins with this: Making the act agreeable to an apprentice—unless you are content to date among your own sort.

The Golden Shower

Let us take, as an example, the "water sport" known as the "golden shower"—sex play with urine. Once the tactful tinkler has established their partner's interest in sailing the urine seas, they must make it their constant care to render smooth sailing. If, for example, the novice finds the smell off-putting, the tactful tinkler should drink water excessively— the clearer the stream, the less pungent the bouquet (besides, the well-bred citizen knows that eight glasses a day is just good, healthy living). A gentleman or lady never expects the rainstorm to take place on the novice's sheets. The tactful tinkler invests in a vinyl mattress cover, or simply holds the flow until in the shower or the great outdoors. It is impertinent to expect the novice to spoon until both parties have showered (or at least baby-wiped).

If the initial attempt is successful, it is gauche to request it again twelve hours later. The tactful tinkler makes it clear they are open to suggestion at all hours, and then lets the novice decide when, where, and

how much. Should the novice agree
to do it more than once every two or
three weeks, then marry the creature—for that, ladies and gentlemen, is love.

Foot Admiration

Pity the poor foot fetishist, he is
much maligned in society. Otherwise
open-minded ladies and gentlemen
look askance at foot appreciation.
But it is ill-mannered and ignorant to stereotype the admirer as

Returning the Favor

It cannot be too strongly
insisted upon that the
fetishist practice reci-
procity. A well-mannered
citizen discovers what
kinky, quirky act their
otherwise vanilla lover
has always wanted to
indulge in and honors it unconditionally—
even if that means taking tea with the
in-laws sans underwear once a week so
you can be flagellated with a cat o' nine
tails.

an adult nerd or a misunderstood "freak"—as if he were socially awkward, even a bit touched in the head. No longer is it permissible
to follow the curious old-fashioned custom of gossiping about the lady
or gentleman with "a bit of a foot thing." It is gauche to pass on the
rumor that he never saw much action in high school save for that one
time Tammy Mixler sprained her ankle in gym class and the fetishist-in-
training helped carry her to the nurse's office.

It is perfectly correct to admire the foot more so than, say, the elbow.
The gentleman or lady who subverts the foot when they walk in the bedroom does not deserve all the nerve endings they are blessed with down
there. And the lady who crams her tootsies into crippling Manolo Blahniks
and then refuses to treat her feet as sexual objects deserves a mean case
of calluses. The lover who is quick to dismiss this territory simply because
it lies so far from all the hot genital action will never know how much
pleasure the feet can receive—and give. It is unbecoming to avoid the
feet simply because your grandmother once asked you to give her tired
old soles a good rub and you could feel her corns and bony toes through

her woolen socks. A well-groomed lady or gentleman knows that callused corners, a faint gorgonzola aroma, and hairy toes can all be easily dealt with via a quick pumice scrub in the shower, one sweep with a shaver, and a rubdown with lotion specially formulated for the piggies (good old Dr. Scholl's will suffice).

FANTASY ISLAND

Nothing discovers a small mind more than publicly judging another based on his or her fantasy. The boor who would act as the sexual thought police does not deserve to be thought of sexually. Nor should you yourself edit the contents of your own fantasies in an effort to make them "normal"— to do so is as preposterous as censoring your own diary, and only the pretentious sorts who fancy themselves memoirists do that. Your fantasy life is your own private, triple-bolted sex lair and what you lodge there is no one's business but your own. The habit of retreating there is to be encouraged. If there is no likelihood of your fantasy negatively impacting your relationship, your job, or how often you call your mother or dust your room, then it is beyond reproof.

The well-mannered lady or gentleman knows that thinking on a thing, no matter how much one enjoys thinking on it, does not mean one wishes to act on it. Children are permitted to have active, colorful imaginations, and modern lovers would do well to recall those times. Does a small child fret that their Little Orphan Annie fantasy means they actually wish their parents dead? The urbane adult does not sacrifice the daydream for the day job. It is no longer fashionable to hold forth on how daydreaming means one is not content with one's lot, or how fantasizing means one is not happy with one's lover. The lady or gentleman who has banished such antiquated notions will experience the joy of adding a salacious slant to that make-believe adoption fantasy. *Now* who's your daddy?

Only the stuffy resist exploring areas that in the mind they would never actually venture into. One's everyday sex life might be compassed by jealousy, insecurity, fear of STDs, fear of embarrassment, fear of the law, fear of your parents walking in, fear of heights. Or perhaps it is governed by a strict moral code, strict sexual preferences, or strict monogamy agreements. But a fantasy life is not impeded by such fears or limited by such ethics. Your fantasy need not even abide by the laws of physics.

Taboos are sexy; breaking them—as long as no laws are breached in the process—is sexier. To break a *self-imposed* taboo is to experience the full capacity of your fantasy life: We may frown upon acts we experience only in our minds, but the fact that the acts make us frown is part of their appeal. A fantasy may be counterintuitive to the lady or gentleman you present yourself as in society. For instance, a feminist may fantasize about bending over a carburetor dressed in cheesy, scratchy lingerie with her hair teased, sprayed, and back-combed in the tackiest of styles. This is perfectly correct, for one's fantasies should not be bound by "politically correct" mores. And no, seemingly hypocritical kinks do not necessarily reflect deep-seated repression, neuroses, or issues. As with dreams, fantasies may be inspired by something as shallow as the previous evening's television lineup or that summer's trashy beach reading (no matter what Freud said).

Of course, it is the complete dullard who attempts to cordon off daily stresses and relationship quibbles from one's sex drive and sexual preferences. The intermingling is as normal as that of the peas and mashed potatoes. A lady or gentleman's fantasy might be a means of balancing the scales of control and submission. A cliché, perhaps, but it would be obnoxiously self-righteous to refuse to get off on a cliché—that is simply one more incentive to disobey. Guilt has no right intruding on your fantasy life—though the modern gentleman or lady knows that as an *occasional* guest, guilt can be titillating company.

To deny yourself an orgasm is a gross injustice. The well-mannered citizen remembers that orgasms (and especially a lady's Os) are not to be found growing on trees. It is not inelegant to take them in whatever form they arrive. Ladies are often in particular want of assistance—it is neither unbecoming nor untruthful, in such cases, for them to imagine a scenario to bring their genitals up to speed. A true lady lets her mind go to its naughty place, knowing that her body will follow. Neither ladies nor gentlemen should consider their own fantasies too off-color, or trifling, or mediocre, or grotesque—it is far more becoming to accept them just the way they are, in all their fucked-up glory, and simply enjoy them.

Entertaining a Guest on Fantasy Island

True courtesy naturally dictates that you share at least some of your fantasies with a long-term partner—and especially so if you are a frequent fantasizer. It is not necessary to rush this process—share only those fantasies you see fit to share, and do not feel pressed to share anything if you do not love and trust your partner. If your partner does not run screaming from the boudoir, then he or she is deserving of dinner. And should your partner help you fulfill your fantasy, at least a little, then he or she is deserving of a marriage proposal. Herein, the basic rules of etiquette for sharing a fantasy:

- Fantasizing about one's ex is permissible (though no more than once a month); sharing this fantasy with one's current partner is not.
- Fantasizing during sex with a partner is to be encouraged, and it is not necessary to share either the fantasy or the fact that one is fantasizing. However, if one is a chronic fantasizer and is unable to share a single scenario with one's long-term partner, it is, perhaps, a cause for concern.
- It is ungracious to encourage a partner to share their fantasy and then take issue with it. If you cannot handle the truth, then do not request it.

- The well-bred citizen knows how to share a fantasy with tact. It is what Miss Manners (the original etiquette doyenne) calls "polite fiction." If your partner is particularly sensitive about the size of his member, for example, it would be impudent to mention the super-schlong on your fantasy gentleman. Et cetera, et cetera.

- A gentleman or lady never *admits* to fantasizing about their partner's parents or siblings. First cousins, however, are permissible conversation fodder at art-gallery openings.

- Every lady and gentleman desires to be someone else's fantasy. Therefore, it is a gracious gesture to acknowledge masturbating while thinking of your partner—but only after three months of dating. If you have never thought of your sweetheart while rubbing one out, it is recommended you try it at least once—if only so you can share the complimentary news.

The Reluctant Role-Player

It is reasonable to be suspicious of a lady or gentleman who is *too* comfortable getting into character or costume. It brings to mind medieval festivals or, worse, drama majors. When one is role-playing with a new partner for the first time, it is objectionable to run to the closet, grab one's five-piece cowboy outfit (complete with lasso) and yell, "Ready, pardner?" An outfit that has been worn with a previous partner should only be worn after six months of dating, or after four brand-new role-playing scenarios, whichever comes first.

The well-mannered lover knows that it takes two to role-play, and that a gentleman's ultimate fantasy might be a lady's ultimate nightmare. The Catholic schoolgirl scenario, for example (see The Lady Wears Plaid on p. 135), arouses salacity in approximately 87 percent of modern heterosexual gentlemen—whereas ladies might not get quite so hot and bothered recalling their teenage acne, their mortification the day their breasts sprouted, or their junior prom date who said he would "be right

back" during a slow dance and left them standing there solo for the remainder of "In Your Eyes." (Manners for the junior set would have made
many a prom more bearable.) The lady might prefer a lascivious house-
wife/paper-delivery boy scenario—though she should be sensitive to any
bullying and name-calling her partner may have suffered on his 5 A.M.
paper route in sixth grade.

Repressed preteen trauma aside, there are numerous benefits to con-
quering stage fright in the bedroom. The people who can be pleasantly
silly in the sack and who have a knack for talking dirty (or simply talking
in character) are generally a delight to sleep with. Sex thrives on such
butterflies. It is wise to remember that rational conversation and political debate are quite out of place during such merry times—unless they
are part of your scene.

The most important point of role-play etiquette is that a lady and
gentleman adhere to a strict quid pro quo policy. They do not have to
agree on every scenario, but they should take turns calling the shots (and
picking the outfits). Remember, one's fantasy is one's prerogative, no
matter how hackneyed. If you dig deep enough, most people have something trite hidden on their own private fantasy island. Besides, it is outmoded and ignorant to believe that enacting a fantasy with a beau in
costume means you want to do it in real life. A fantasy is no more than an
idea that is pleasing to you, a taboo that is sexy to break—often in the
only place it is legal: your own head (well, there and Mississippi). It is ill-
tempered to dismiss a partner's fantasy outright, no matter how banal
you find it. In fact, it is ill-tempered to dismiss outright *anything* someone requests in bed, assuming they ask nicely. You are not bound to agree
to anything, of course, but you should stifle your reproof and be a good
listener. When someone confesses to a sexual preference, it is an act of
bravery—if you laugh haughtily, call them a boor, or wonder aloud how
any well-bred citizen could find that remotely appealing, the confessor is
less likely to speak up next time. Which is lamentable, because their next
fantasy might have been a prodigious one. It is churlish not to take plea-

sure in the simple fact that your beau shared something intimate with you.

That said, only the lout presses their partner to take part in a fantasy he or she is uncomfortable with. And it is unforgivably barbaric to make the confession of a fantasy an indictment of your beau's real-life sexual persona ("Honey, I've always fantasized about women with double Ds, and your tits are too small. Would you be a dear and get implants?"). However, we can think of nary a fantasy so off-color that two happily consenting partners should not try it at least once. Lovers would do well to remember that not every sexual act has to get both partners off equally. Sometimes a thing is worth doing just because it excites your partner—and few things are more agreeable than seeing someone you love overwhelmed by lust due to something you said/wrote/wore/sang/licked.

It is common to encounter feelings of embarrassment or self-consciousness when role-playing for the first time, but this is no guarantee the encounter will not have a salacious end for you both. Even the most accomplished actors feel nauseated before opening night, but once the curtain rises, they feel there is no place they would rather be. Of course, if *both* parties feel stiff and inelegant in full medieval garb or doctor and nurse uniforms, then that may hinder a horny time for all. But if, perchance, one of you finds the scenario sexy, that can be enough to mitigate the other's overwhelming feeling of "Oh my God I look like a horse's ass."

If you can banish the notion that this is silly, anything is possible. It is not necessary to be the theatrical type just to play along, though many a lady and gentleman have found that once in costume, they feel a little more, well, theatrical. When one does not feel quite oneself, it is immeasurably easier to say things that would normally be out of character (which is why, sadly, so many less-refined ladies and gentlemen rely on getting soused to get into character). Ultimately, the one who chose the scenario is responsible for maintaining the mood. If a lady asks a gentleman to don a sweater vest and hold a clipboard, he is not required to convince her he is her driving school instructor—he simply wears the outfit, and her dirty mind will fill in the gaps.

The Lady Wears Plaid

Few schoolboys bed as many schoolgirls as they would like. Some compensate by making a grand entrance at their ten-year high school reunion, while others know it is not necessary to wait. It is perfectly acceptable for a gentleman to make amends in his fantasy life by wanking to Britney's "Oops! I Did It Again" video. (Though in some cases, a gentleman's recurring schoolgirl fantasy may be motivated by a simple love of plaid.)

Of course, a lady is within her rights to find the thought of donning a Catholic school uniform while sucking on a Blow Pop a tad distasteful. But the gracious lady finds a compromise that will suit her beau's fantasy. When full regalia

The Innocent Bystander

A gentleman or lady does not insist on sharing fantasies in polite company—it is exhausting and embarrassing to listen to an acquaintance's extended (and often mediocre) dream sequence. In much the same way, it is vulgar to make your fellow citizens unwitting players in your scenario. It is perfectly correct for a couple to venture into public in character, mind you, as long as it does not inconvenience others. It is not uncouth to have the lady wear a hidden vibrator while the gentleman carries the remote, for example. It is, however, intolerable to create embarrassment for perfect (and perfectly nice) strangers. For example, some couples in power-play scenarios have been known to incorporate security checks into their games: The gentleman's humiliation when his nipple clamps and cock ring set off the alarm is all part of the fun. This is vulgar and inelegant behavior—it causes unnecessary delays for your fellow passengers and involves the security officers in your scene without their consent. A modern lady or gentleman knows that limiting the public scene to simply going commando is a small sacrifice to make for one's country.

would embarrass the lady beyond arousal, props may be substituted. A lady should never underestimate the impact of simple pigtails if the gentleman has a thing for school-girl accoutrements. She may also wear white, knee-high socks and sensible, white, schoolgirl undies beneath her gown. Or she may wait until Halloween.

The lady is advised that if she plays along with her gentleman's schoolgirl fantasy just once—and just once is all prudence demands—she should be sure to milk it for all it's worth. She should recall how much she used to make out as a young girl, back when the code of conduct dictated that it was too soon for adult sex. She should reminisce over the time spent dallying at second and third bases. She should remember the hickeys. The well-bred lover will recognize these acts as foreplay—and even the most refined citizen could use a little more of this. Hence, the lady should be the prudish schoolgirl and make her boyfriend work for it. This time, he has to talk her into sex. In her short, plaid skirt (or even just in pigtails), she is no longer a sure thing.

PRISTINE POTTY TALK

We know a lovely lady of leisure who found herself one evening on a third date with a charming, if somewhat reserved young gentleman. There they were, before a roaring fire in the hearth, on their second bottle of a delightful syrah and grenache blend: shoes off, fingers entwined, end credits rolling on the video. They teetered on the precipice between friendship and something more for a moment, before our lady friend leaned in gracefully and the tonsil-hockey ensued. Heavy breathing quickly turned into sighs, sighs into moans, moans into a few inspired "ohs" and "ahs." Then, like a Klaxon horn to her ear, a flurry of words began to pour forth from her lover's lips so appalling, so unconscionable, we dare not mention them by name. And yet, how can we resist? Indeed! "Aaaaw yeah, baby, your booty's like two ice-cream scoops I'm gonna lick until you melt in my mouth, my little banana split."

Dirty talk always looks atrocious on paper, and it is not always pleasing to the ear in person. That is because bedroom banter is as individual as musical taste. One may pass muster by speaking with confidence and conviction, and one may sustain him or herself in the moment by never breaking character, but if one's kinky sensibilities be not perfectly in sync with those of his or her lover, then one's potty mouth will surely be the main source of amusement round that lover's watercooler tomorrow morn. Just as you must choose your words with the utmost care when introduced to someone whose ivories you would like to tickle, so too must you speak with at least a modicum of thoughtfulness when actually tickling those ivories—even if only four-letter words are to be employed. You can make a sailor blush, so as long as you do not make your lover suffer an incurable case of the giggles.

Of course, what is sexy to one is often ludicrous to another. But you may increase your chances of eliciting a favorable response to your verbal filth no matter who your audience by following a few simple rules. For inspiration, do not rely solely on those two biggest advocates of *fromage* and cliché: pornography and R&B. So formulaic, so predictable, they teach us nothing about subtlety, imagination, or creative euphemism. Cunning linguists would do well to use new and varied role models, in the tradition of DH Lawrence, John Donne, and Liz Phair. Whoever you channel, remember to start slowly, customize your script to match your particular partner's needs, and say it loudly and proudly. And for sex's sake, dear friend, enlist the aid of a thesaurus.

Do not censor yourself too rigidly, though, for the only thing worse than an overly cocksure conversationalist is a tentative talker ("Your . . . uh . . . your . . . that is so . . . wet/big"). Speak freely, but keep the number of special requests disguised as dirty talk to a minimum, especially with new partners you wish to bed again, lest they be made to feel inadequate or tyrannized. And do be careful not to automatically assume

No lady or gentleman will be guilty of the vulgarity of masturbating during a phone call without the express and enthusiastic permission of the party on the other end of the line.

your partner embraces the philosophy that anything may be muttered in the throes of passion without consequence: feelings could be hurt, mis-interpretations made. An enthusiastic "Fuck, I love you!" screamed at the top of your lungs for all the angels of Heaven to hear while you climax may feel good to you in the moment, but it may break your partner's heart when he or she realizes only months later that you were speaking from organs other than the heart.

We are loathe to delineate suitable vocabulary for cupidity—after all, so much of dirty talk is about context. However, there are some words for certain body parts that are more prone to evoke laughter, offense, or re-vulsion when uttered in the heat of passion than others. Use the chart on p. 140 to determine the level of risk you may be taking by using one par-ticular euphemism over another. Where exactly each term falls in the chart has been determined by a complex formula that weighs the fol-lowing factors: originality, number of syllables, excessive poetry, how easily it rolls off the tongue, direct-ness verses coyness, et cetera. You will note in most cases, the greater number of words to a term, the higher the risk. Of course, this is not an ex-act science, so use your judgment. When in doubt, simply say your part-ner's name: So long as you get it right, what lady or gentlemen could take offense to that?

Erotic Letters

So long as it does not jeopardize your part-ner's standing at their place of business, it is not inappropriate to send them lascivious notes throughout the day—whether via email, instant messaging, text messaging, video messaging, voice mail, et cetera—as a preview of marvelous things to come, as it were. Be sure to be discreet while com-posing letters, as well as whenever perus-ing them. Of course, one must keep in mind that anything done in excess is likely to suffer a degradation in novelty. Avoid wearing out this practice like a favorite pair of dress shoes by sending your notes not willy-nilly, but deliberately.

VIRTUOUS VOYEURISM

No lady should permit a gentleman to be so familiar with her as to shoot her in the nude if she does not trust him with the negatives. And no gentleman should press a lady to disrobe for his camera if he has not yet earned her trust. When a gentleman inquires, "May I shoot you nude?" he probably means—assuming he is, indeed, a true gentleman—"Your beauty astounds me and I wish to record it for posterity." But what the lady probably hears is, "The theme of the next guys' night out is Show-and-Tell," or, "I've heard amateur porn sites are a great way to make some fast cash." All men are not gentlemen, and many a man has been known to show his friends dirty pictures of a lovesick maiden he once kicked to the curb.

First, a couple must establish ground rules. If a gentleman has proven himself trustworthy (by being always forthright and faithful), then his ladyfriend might just believe his vow to share the photographs with no one besides his right hand. But the lady is well within her rights to demand a little more convincing—after all, there are some ill-mannered and malicious amateur pornographers masquerading as beaus, who take pleasure in misleading ladies with false promises. (It is enough simply to mention such impertinence in order to despise it as we ought.) A well-mannered gentleman will not balk at a lady's hesitations. Instead, he will promise her custody of all photographs and negatives—he will profess that he is content simply to visit them on occasion. Or he will suggest they use a Polaroid camera—no negatives! (Besides, a Polaroid flatters everyone.) A *truly* elegant gentleman will offer to pose naked for his lady. In fact, a gentleman who is not willing to disrobe does not deserve to have his request honored. And if a lady is not captivated by this suggestion in the slightest—if she expresses not an iota of interest in capturing her gentleman in the buff—then she does not deserve said gentleman. Whatever promises the gentleman makes to convince a lady to disrobe he is required to keep—even if she dumps him for his butler.

	LOW RISK	MEDIUM RISK	HIGH RISK
Terms for Vagina	mon petit bijou, je ne sais quoi, sweetness, cunt*	pussy, peachfish, monster, Virginia (or any first name), box, fig, puss, puswa, pussywillow, honey pot, downtown, cooch, coochie, wana, the pink, quim, fun bits, holy of holies, tender conch shell, angel hole, janer, little devil, pie, cock, cunny, china, graceland, cookie, muffin, cha-cha, her, my girl, v.g., veegee, muff, peach, love glove, love silo, love cup kitty, princess	yoni, twat, penis cozy, womanhood, verticle smile, nest, slip-n-slide, slip-inside, slot, red river valley, creamline, cooter, pleasure pie, incubator (dinkubator when filled), vadge, vagina, snatch, cream-n-sugar festering axe wound, and any words or phrases that imply a bad smell or taste—the only excuse for using such terms is if you are a fifth grader or an imbecile
Terms for Penis	Cock, dick, sweet Jesus, penis,	pud, junk, dong, sword, bone, wood, rod, pull toy, knob, fountain, probe, coke, root, shaft, stick, firestarter, love nuggets (testes)	ding-a-ling, putz, cock-a-doodle, hoo hoo, rumpled foreskin, sushi roll, a baby's arm holding an apple, pig in a blanket (for the unmaimed), dollywhacker, Mr. Happy, one-eyed wonder-worm, love

*The word "cunt" may have a low, medium, or high risk factor for offense, depending on the politics of the owner of the cunt, the geographic region in which the term is spoken, the use of the term by the speaker in nonsexual situations, and the grammatic elegance of the sentence is which it is used.

	LOW RISK	MEDIUM RISK	HIGH RISK
Terms for Penis (continued)			pump, meat muscles, jimmy, wang chung, joint, tallywhacker, skeleton key, third leg, prick, spike, purple-headed paratrooper of passion, willy, the incredible mallet of danger, tube steak, twig and berries, mushroom of love, flesh torpedo, skin flute, pocket rocket, trouser snake, crank, scud, love weasel, squishy cigar, dagger of love, dong, willy, trouser snake, Mr. Pokey or "Mr." anything, lingam, throbbing bratwurst, super spewer, tally-whacker, tickle stick, gorgon, heat-seeking moisture missile, peter, pistol, pokey, punk, baloney pony, dork, pee pee, winky, sweet potato, the magic lamp, purple-helmeted warrior of love, the savage beast, the clam spear

But perhaps the lady's (or even the gentleman's) concerns about being captured on film are more aesthetic. It is not uncommon for the most comely maiden or exquisite young man to find their own image disagreeable. Which is just one more reason why a gentleman and lady should compliment each other daily—if your first compliment of the season is, "You're a total babe, can I take some nudies?" it may

Make a Spectacle of the Lady

A gentleman who encounters resistance when attempting to shoot his lady should remember this: A lady is more likely to believe you just want to capture her beauty *en totale* if your manor is already decorated with images of her fully-clothed—on the fridge, nightstand, desk, et cetera.

be received as lecherous rather than laudatory. The polite pornographer promises to destroy any images that capture their partner's mythical back fat. The modern couple may choose to use a digital camera so they can delete as they go, while experimenting with positions and lighting. There is one thing that should always be remembered by those who aspire to amateur photography, which is, never shoot from below in order to avoid amplifying or in some cases creating a double or even triple chin. In fact, as a general rule of etiquette, if we all stopped shooting each other from below, the world would be a more agreeable place.

SPANKING WITH APLOMB

A spank can excite or it can irritate, it can be salacious or simply ridiculous. Many a lovemaking session has deteriorated into giggles as a result of a boneless hand extended to the rump as though it were a boiled fish or a used condom. Of course, one does not wish to leave unwelcome marks, and giggles are not entirely unwelcome—a little frivolity is to be expected in the bedroom. A thoroughly staid and solemn approach to sex is an anachronism: If we are not able to laugh at our foibles and fumblings, then our behavior will be circumscribed by a fear of looking silly, and we will never try anything new. As, for instance, spanking. There are certain rules of etiquette that will help you spank with grace, to ensure you leave a red, hand mark as distinctive, yet subtle, as the most elegant of calling cards.

- There is no fixed guideline for when spanking is apropos—the rule is elastic, depending on how experimental your sex life is, and how much the lady or gentleman enjoys surprises. Prudence suggests you ascertain your partner's attitude toward spanking before laying on a hand in the midst of deep—eye contact, lovey-dovey missionary sex. However, if the session has already evolved into hair-pulling, biting, wrestling sex, then a spank will feel more at home.
- How hard one should spank depends on the pain/pleasure threshold of the spankee. However, remember that there is a wide distance between rudeness and reserve. If in doubt, the spanker should initially err on the side of reserve, and gradually build up to rudeness. However, timid or hesitant spanks are gaucheries to be avoided.
- While the spank need not be reserved for the ass alone, the consummate spanker knows to focus attention on *fleshy* body parts and carefully avoids joints, bones, spine, backs of the knees, and lower thighs.
- It should go without saying—though, of course, if anything went without saying, there would be no need for etiquette manuals—that spanking belongs in a respectful, loving relationship. One must practice perfect manners outside the bedroom, making consideration and gentleness an integral part of one's behavior, and then, one is permitted to spank with abandon.
- The tactful spankee who desires to be whacked with more gusto does not say, "You spank like a girl, you big wuss." The tactful spankee rather phrases the request as a desire for more, i.e., "Harder, big boy."

- The tactful spankee who desires to be whacked with less gusto should simply say so.
- The tactful spankee who desires not to be whacked at all should switch positions or suggest something new to avoid dropping the curtain on the entire session.
- The consummate spanker does not say, "Oh, I'm sorry!" or, "Did that hurt?" The consummate spanker *does* say, in the aftermath, "May I kiss it better?"

A Blush upon Thy Cheek

Even more taboo (and therefore risky) than the spank to the bottom is the slap to the face. The tush, after all, can seem so far removed from our true identity, while the cheek is in immediate proximity to the very windows of our souls. If bottom spanking is kinky ha-ha, then face slapping is serious kinky. Therefore, we can only condone the latter activity when someone has expressly requested it. Once given permission, you must find the delicate balance between conviction and gentle- ness in this arena, it is always better to a limp-palmed pat rather than something more vigorous. Remember, you can always work up to a greater sting upon the urging of your partner. Use the utmost care to avoid the eyes, ears, and nose. And never attempt to leave a mark upon your lover's visage: He or she may get off on it, but you may get your derriere thrown into prison.

CHAPTER V
Love and War

It would be foolish to hold that manners were meant to govern solely the interactions of strangers (or near strangers). Only the ignorant believe that politesse is simply a veneer of kindness, and that what lies beneath should not be regulated. On the contrary, dear readers, to forget our manners when we are in love (or even at war) would be as rude as neglecting to acknowledge an old friend's birthday simply because "he already knows I care." Whether your relationship is as comfortable, familiar, and well-worn as a favorite pair of slippers *or* falling apart at the seams, well-bred citizens always see fit to behave.

LONG-TERM RELATIONSHIPS (LTRS)

Manners should not be forsaken in a long-term relationship (LTR), but rather redressed for the situation. It is vulgar to become lazy about politesse, though we would not be so stiff as to suggest that conversation and behavior over dinner in the ninth month should mimic that on the first date. Manners serve to remind us that we are indeed fortunate to be in love—because once we start to take a partner for granted and let our dedication to courtesy wane, the relationship is well-nigh history.

Communication

The gentleman or lady always spits it out. No, not *that*, dirty birds. We are, of course, referring to those things called "words," which one may string together in a variety of ways to form "sentences" that can miraculously convey one's innermost thoughts. It is called "com-mun-i-cation," and it works wonders. However, it takes practice and a delicate touch to form sentences that will yield mind-blowing oral sex instead of the silent treatment. If what you wish to discuss is both salacious and also delicate—perchance you fancy exploring a heretofore untouched orifice—it is advisable to conduct the conversation outside of the bedroom, so no one feels judged (on what just happened) or pressured (on what is about to happen). If you simply cannot bring it up over the crème brûlée, then you may try talking immediately *after* sex, when things are fresh in your mind and you are both (one would hope) more relaxed. (For more on awkward conversations, see p. 200.)

If you are unsure how your partner is feeling, it is only polite to open up your mouth and ask. If you are not sure how your partner likes their sex, it is only polite to open up your mouth and ask. If you would like your partner to know how you are feeling or how you like your sex, it is only polite to open up your mouth and tell them (nicely, please).

In addition, the gentleman or lady always laps it up. No, not *that*, cheeky monkeys. It is of utmost importance to reward good communication by actually listening to what your partner is saying, absorbing the advice, and acting upon it. And the gentleman or lady does not assume that acting on it once is sufficient, unless they find the act entirely disagreeable, in which case they must, of course, say so.

At times, however, even the most civilized gentleman or lady may find the words catching in their throat. If you simply do not know how to address the subject, it is acceptable to confide in a friend—in fact, it is always acceptable to test-drive a particularly difficult conversation with a close, trusted friend. It is unforgivably vulgar, however, to harp on about a problem in public without ever sharing your concerns with your partner. If it is troubling you so, it is unfair not to give your sweet one a chance to make amends, make changes, or make a move for the door. The only ex-

I Love You! Good God I Love You!

The civilized gentleman or lady does not say "I love you" for the first time during sex unless it is truly meant. In the case of such an outburst, it is elegant to repeat the sentiment as soon after the sex as possible, to reassure the loved one it was indeed sincere. However, if the expression was no more than an orgasmic blunder blurted in the throes of passion, and you are not yet prepared to repeat yourself outside the bedroom, then it is advisable not to mention it again and keep your lips buttoned during all subsequent sessions. The only exception to this rule is if the outburst occurs over casual sex or a one-night stand, during which instance it is acceptable to make a joke of your misfiring synapses. When you do announce your *true* love properly, you would do well to speak clearly and loudly so your partner is not left wondering whether you simply feel a deep fondness for female sheep, or the stew you ordered for your entrée. If you are unsure whether or not your partner uttered those three, sweet words, it is prudent to assume they did not. Sometimes our heart plays tricks upon our ears, and looking for confirmation of what we *want* to hear more often than not leads to disappointment and painfully awkward moments. For those of you who bandy about the term willy-nilly, you would do well to exhibit some restraint, lest you inadvertently degrade the term's meaning and impact. For example, the habit of announcing that one "loves the new John Grisham novel" is quite gauche. Finally, if nine months have passed and there has not been either an "I love you" or rimming, consider moving on.

ception to this rule concerns temporary outbursts on trifling matters—sometimes it is enough simply to vent to a good friend that your partner never shuts off the light in the bathroom, never deletes the junkmail in the inbox, never phrases *Jeopardy!* answers in the form of a question. Matters as weightless as these need not be shared—unless you find them *truly* vexing.

It is inelegant to joke about kids in your future unless you are either partially serious or on a one-night stand. You may express your level of seriousness via the number of kids you openly fantasize about: A two-child fantasy is infinitely more serious than joking about what good-looking septuplets you would produce together.

Remembering the Niceties

In the early stages of dating, one expects compliments—almost to the point of not hearing them. They are uttered as foreplay, they are extended as feelers of the romantic vibe, they are as much a dating convention as dinner-and-a-movie. How much more impact, then, can a compliment have in a long-term relationship? Once the two of you are each other's sure things, it is the purest form of flattery. Only the vulgar long-term companion withholds compliments until he or she requires something (your help moving a heavy object, your company at dinner with a tiresome coworker, your tongue on their chocolate starfish). The elegant gentleman or lady compliments their long-term partner at least once a day—if only to remind *themselves* how blessed they are to wake up next to such an exquisite creature each morning. In particular, if one's partner is a gentleman, one should resolve to tell that gentleman how one admires the size, shape, and personality of his member at least once a month. If one's partner is a lady, it is elegant to compliment her bosom and behind at least as often as one squeezes them.

If a gentleman or lady cannot muster a compliment on a particular day (perhaps you are feeling sorry for yourself or slightly narcissistic), then at the very least, you should remember to say please, thank you, and excuse me (or *excusez moi* if you are confident of pulling it off with flair). Our world would be a more habitable place if we were all more generous with these terms. However, it is unspeakably vulgar to misuse these words and utter them as insults; to bark out "Excuse me!" as one barges past a stranger on the subway is the height of passive-aggressive rudeness.

Finally, the elegant gentleman or lady always attempts to live up to a compliment rather than sink into it. If you wanted to look your best for someone on the third date, how much more should you want to do so now that you are in love? It is not necessary—in fact, it is quite clownish—to wear makeup or a toupee to bed, but it is graceless to completely abandon one's workout routine simply because one is no longer competing on the open market. Commitment is not a free pass to slobbery. For appropriate behavior when one's partner attempts to use such a free pass, see p. 207.

Keeping the Mystery: Finding a Balance Between Intimacy and TMI

In these modern times, when Broadway musicals are named after human-waste fluids and mainstream Hollywood comedies feature A-list actresses with very masculine fluids in their hair, it can be difficult to determine where the line falls between intimacy and TMI (too much information). While we would like nothing more than to draw that line for you, it is an endeavor that must be undertaken by each individual couple. However, there is one rule by which *all* couples must abide: The partner who requires slightly *less* information prevails. No matter if you have always enjoyed an open flatulence policy with your exes, if your current beau would rather not "pull your finger," then you must acquiesce. For some ladies and gentleman, an ill-timed episode of wind can be heartbreaking—it indicates to them that you no longer respect them, that the steamy sex and romantic glances are about to yield to burps at breakfast and fart jokes in the dining room.

It *is* acceptable, however, to gently, *elegantly* nudge at a slightly prim partner's boundaries, especially after six or more months of dating. Breaking down walls is part of the fun of long-term relationships. However, the

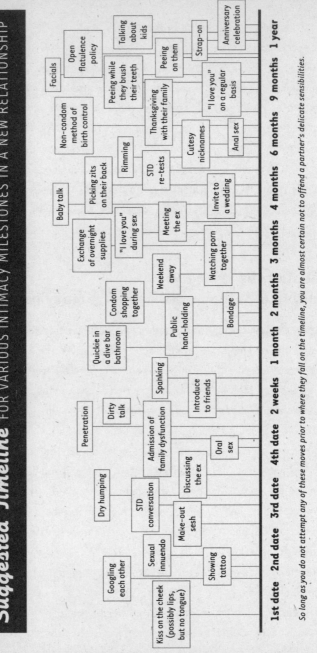

gentleman or lady knows that hollering "Come check out this awesome doodie I just made!" does not constitute a gentle, elegant nudge. Nor does barging in on your partner while they are making their own doodie, especially if they are in the habit of shutting the door behind them. For some, the bathroom is a private zone of concentration, reflection, and embarrassing hair removal. To invade such a personal space disrespects a person's right to privacy, as well as their right to maintain a little mystery and allure.

Will You Be My Best Friend Forever (BFF)?

All you need is love. Love is a potent salve to heal all wounds. Love is spackle to plug all emotional holes. All I need is the air that I breathe and to love you. Listen up, ladies and gentlemen, lest you suddenly find yourself the proud owner of ten acres of swampland in Florida: This is poppycock!

It is a somewhat modern notion that the requirements of Love with a capital *L* include myriad responsibilities: Not only do you have to be a lover, but also a best friend with a degree in emotional therapy, a knack for business, and a penchant for interior design. Even more agreeable if you can cook, too. But it is ignorant to expect one's long-term partner to fill every one of these roles—not even the most refined lady or gentleman is capable of all this. It is a wonder more people do not burn out on this "Love," growing ever more resentful of the people they have to be for their partners in the name of love, rather than being the people they want to be in the name of self-preservation.

It is ill-advised to expect one's partner to fill this many roles, lest one be disappointed—or worse, under duress, tempted to cheat on that partner. The gentleman and lady who expect to be all things to each other will have to agree on taste in movies, on reproductive rights, on how offspring should be raised, on how the toilet paper should be installed, on how food should be chewed, on the best position for boot-knocking, on wallpaper versus paint and carpeting versus hardwood floors, on Freud, on politics, on pop music.

And if "little things mean a lot," as that other love song professes, then those little things can nibble away at romance's delicate foundation just as much as they can build it up. Insidious, annoying, daily habits become the grim reapers of love. Because, dear readers, nine times out of ten, "irreconcilable differences" is just a fancy legal term for incompatible music taste. Gentlemen and ladies bent on long-term monogamy should therefore bowl often with a buddy, keep the butler and therapist on staff, take ladies' (or gentlemen's) golf weekends away, and above all, make sure their best friend is someone other than their spouse.

Sexual History Lessons

No longer is it permissible to follow yesteryear's custom of judging a gentleman or lady on the number of sexual partners in their past. Hence, should you ask your partner to detail their sexual history—not as it relates to STDs, because, as civilized beings, you already had that conversation before hopping into bed—you must be prepared to handle it with aplomb. Nothing is more inelegant than a partner who demands, "Tell me everything," when what they *really* mean to say is, "Please lie in order to placate my ego and my outmoded notions of ladylike/gentlemanly behavior." Gentlemen in particular are wont to be troubled when their ladyfriend's little black book resembles the yellow pages. The madonna/whore complex has been around for as long as men have been sleeping with madonnas and whores: The men who suffer from it care little where a lady has been so long as they do not care where she is *going*, but the moment they start to imagine a future with her in it, they wish her to become a born-again virgin. Such gentlemen should be careful to walk with their hands in their pockets lest they scrape their knuckles on the ground.

Gentlemen and ladies alike are wont to frown upon what they consider to be an excessive amount of *casual* sex on their partner's relationship resume. It is hard for persons of very strong moral convictions not to impose them upon others, especially those whom they love. (Think anti-abortionists, Jehovah's Witnesses, us.) The combination of love and sex is certainly a prodigious one, but only the neophyte believes a strict, life-long adherence to it is a relationship requirement. In addition, it is insolent to expect a partner to disclaim their past like so much flotsam. By the same token, it is vulgar in the extreme to don a vizard of purity in a relationship and act as if one has no sexual history to speak of. People of breeding and true refinement know that a partner's past, no matter how lurid, is part of what makes him or her the creature they currently adore. It is correct to recognize that everyone has the ability to grow and change. Just as you forgive a person for cheerleading in high school or listening to Dave Matthews in college, so too do you accept the fact that they may not be able to recall the names of all the people they once fucked. The simple fact that the two of you now enjoy committed, loving sex should be proof enough of their emotional growth.

The number of past partners should not be an issue—for whether you have slept with one or one hundred people, you may have amassed some amazing sexual maneuvers, some unfortunate infections, or both. It is reminiscent of less enlightened days and highly distasteful to choose an arbitrary number that, once surpassed, guarantees a person a spot in the official Slut Club. Assuming you are always kind, honest, as safe as is technically possible, and thoughtful in your encounters, you may fuck around more than Wilt Chamberlain and still deserve four or five decades of hot monogamy when you finally settle down. A colorful history may indicate nothing more than a healthy libido, and it is certainly not symptomatic of a recreant: If you were generally of sound mind, if you were sober (enough), if you were happy with your lot in life for the most part, if you participated in that kind of sex because you wanted to and not because you were trying to achieve something by it, if *you* never felt shamed by it—then it would be insulting and condescending for another to suggest you *should* be. Listen up, gentle readers: It is not necessary to be blasé about a loved one's past, but it is required that you approach it with humor. Finding amusement in the past is key to a contented existence—or at least to not going utterly insane from unrelenting existential crises.

That all spoken, true courtesy will naturally dictate that you approach this subject with tact and discretion. To brag about one's past is uncouth and excessively unbecoming. What (or should we say *who*) you did in the past is not relevant to your current relationship, but the manner in which you handle it now *is*. You may consider a casual recounting of your casual encounters to be hilarious and benign cocktail-party banter, while your partner may find it crass or even distressing. No matter how blithely someone accepts your sexual history, parley about exes is, as a general rule, irksome. To be comfortable with one's past does not require that one rubs a partner's face in it. While we would all do well to chill the fuck out a little regarding each other's exes, none but a low-bred clown would regale a partner with the unabridged tale of their ex and the mysterious disappearing butt plug. (See p. 177 for more on exes etiquette.)

Jealousy

There are some gentlemen and ladies who believe that the most civilized creatures are capable of banishing jealousy entirely (see Open Relationships on p. 165). Others hold it close, believing that a daily dose of jealousy is essential to long-term fidelity and monogamy. We advise you to avoid the two extremes and learn to live with jealousy as it occurs naturally, neither banishing it completely nor encouraging (or worse, instigating) it.

A *little* bit of jealousy reminds us how precious we consider each other—and how much we have to lose if we do not hold our dear one close. Too much reeks of insecurity, desperation, neediness, and mistrust. The well-bred lady or gentleman knows the difference between holding close

and suffocating, between endearing indignation and petty possessiveness. For example, if our partner is *never* jealous, it makes us wonder, Do
they not care? For while it is acceptable to rest easy in the confidence
your loved one will not leave you, it is entirely disagreeable to act as
if this were a right rather than a privilege. In contrast, if our partner is
always jealous, the green-eyed monster becomes the center of the
relationship, constantly needing to be fed attention.

   In the most elegant of relationships, each partner's restrained jealousy cancels the other's out, pulling the two closer—rather than perpetu-
ally reigniting each other's insecurities, pushing them apart. Ergo, it is
perfectly acceptable to experience displeasure upon discovering naked
pictures of one's partner's ex; it is not acceptable to upload them to the
Internet. It is correct to feel warmly protective when one notices hotties
checking out one's partner; it is not correct to force one's partner to wear
overcoats in August to discourage such attention. It is polite to share
one's feelings of jealousy, so long as one is merely reporting a reaction
rather than accusing a partner of acts taking place only in one's fervid
imagination. On a final note, it is vulgar to provoke jealousy to the extent
that it causes a partner to doubt one's affections. The gentleman or lady
does not mind tempering their behavior slightly if their partner has a
slightly lower-than-average tolerance for flirtatiousness.

Monogamy Matters

Only the barbarian believes that monogamy is something that simply
happens to a relationship. True ladies and gentlemen know it is a decision you make together. Monogamy is not something that simply happens
to *you*, either—if you decide it suits you, it will require some work. If
a lady or gentleman cannot stand the heat of monogamy, they would
do well to get out of the kitchen. But the refined citizen always makes a
dramatic exit—it is intolerable to slink out of the window at night and

slink back in the next morning (for a viable alternative, see Open Relationships on p. 165).

It is vulgar in the extreme to assume that dwindling passion is grounds for giving up on a relationship, as if a fifty-year marriage that is salacious around the clock is even possible. Elegant ladies and gentlemen do not expect to desire congress with their spouse every night of the marriage. They do not expect to look upon their spouse with a lustful appetite every morning they wake beside them. They do not even expect to want to be married every day. As Alan Alda intones in the quintessential couples' film *The Four Seasons*, sometimes you cannot wait for your spouse to walk through the door, and other times just the way they breathe drives you crazy. And as *we* are fond of intoning, you are obliged to endure occasional disagreeable days (or even months) in exchange for having the most agreeable creature with whom to share the majority of your days.

 **Ladies and gentlemen in committed, monogamous relationships should be particular to buttress monogamy rather than put it to the test.**

Stoking the Coals of Monogamy

There may come a time when a disagreeable day or two develops into a dry spell that outlasts the season. It is not correct to simply ignore such a dry spell—the polite lady or gentleman endures hardship, but never ignores it in the hope that it will go away. It is perfectly correct to require physical intimacy in a relationship—it is a legitimate human need (though only vulgarians use this argument if a mere three days have passed since the last rutting). Even the most refined and reserved ladies and gentlemen suffer on a diet of unrequited lust.

As with all aspects of long-term relationships, it is prudent to approach problems together. The polite (and horny) lady or gentleman re-assures their partner that while they do not expect nasty, butt-spankin', porno sex every night of the relationship, some occasional connubial bliss is in order. It is elegant to remind your partner that it is not simply about your own libido—you no doubt miss *giving* pleasure, too.

In addition, lovers who are not in the mood would do well to explain why, as gently as possible, so as not to encourage an inferiority complex in their partner. It is good manners to remind your partner it is not a mat-ter of their relative comeliness, but rather a result of a bad day at work, bad day on the pot, bad day at the altar, et cetera.

Valentine's Day Decorum

We have no gripe with the grinches who consider front-yard Christmas decorations tacky, and we can live in a world with the Serious Christians who find Easter egg hunts inappropriate. But we cannot abide those cold-hearted snakes who use anti-consumerism as an excuse for not celebrating Valentine's Day. If there is one day in the year when we are unwilling to take one in the heart for high-minded lefty-ness, it is Febru-ary 14.

As long as there is a market for blue eye shadow and white stilettos, there will be a market for oversized cards and heart-shaped boxes of in-ferior chocolate. What self-respecting, elegant, downtown dater wishes their relationship to be associated with any of that rubbish? It is un-couth, however, to throw the baby out with the cheap cologne—when you boycott Valentine's, the only person who really suffers is your partner. And while you may feel silly hopping on the romance conveyer belt with the plebes, that is nothing compared with how your intimate friend will feel when asked how they celebrated the "big day." A relationship has a number of perks, prime among them being: a) you have someone to squeeze your bacne; and b) you do not have to feel like an outcast come February. Ladies and gentlemen know that *not* celebrating the holiday will not necessarily send a message to the head honchos at Hallmark, but it *will* send a message to your sweetheart. Gentle readers, it shouts your message! It shouts, "I care so little that I refuse to send a paltry love note on a prepaid postcard! While the rest of the world celebrates the love they have found together, our love does not warrant me lifting a single finger!" This kind of message is odious and unforgivable. A touch of *fromage* goes a long way, no matter what day of the year.

By no means would we suggest you buy a six-foot, pink teddy bear, a heart-shaped box of truffles, or diamond pendant earrings. Consumption as compliment is always uncouth. It is not necessary to spend a dime, but it is required that you spend more than a minute determining the most appropriate way to doff your hat to the relationship, whether you have been together ten

Public Announcements of Affection (PAA)

Public announcements of affection (PAA) can be as unseemly and indecorous as public *displays* of the same, when indulged in without discretion. Do not be continually talking about how "deeply in love" you are or how "soul-melding" the sex is—especially if you have been together for two weeks and are in the habit of serial dating. To harp on about one's current relationship success—especially in the company of one's single friends—is as vulgar as bragging about a holiday bonus from the office. It is especially grotesque to boast loudly of one's good fortune in the sack—your more-discerning friends will be able to read this in the glow of your cheeks and your discreet, generic report that things are dandy. The elegant lady or gentleman knows how to share the good news without making a spectacle. It is not coincidental that the relationships that crash and burn the quickest are frequently those that were once vaunted with the most gusto.

days or ten years. A handmade card (no matter how poorly drawn) will increase your chances of prodigious oral attention later that night more than any piece of jewelry or ten-dollar greeting card that plays The Carpenters' "Close to You" when opened. The gentleman or lady serves breakfast in bed, sends saucy emails all day long, cooks a favorite dinner, draws a bath, lights some candles, plays a favorite album. Other exquisite touches include an hour-long massage with essential oils, a pedicure, a striptease, a picture drawn, a song written, a Rilke poem memorized. Quit that vice you know they hate, hang their photo on your fridge, hold your gas for the evening. Order in pizza and a six-pack of their favorite domestic beer and rent *Mystic Pizza*, if that is their guilty pleasure. Or buy a CD with ocean sounds, make Mai Tais with mini umbrellas, and fill a kiddy pool with warm, soapy water to soak your feet in together. Compliment each other. Count the ways you love each other; count the ways you lust after one another; count to at least one thousand while you administer oral sex. Put your heart in the right place and you will not fail to please.

Masturbation

Masturbation is as fitting an accessory to a long-term relationship as a good port and a wheel of Stilton is to an after-dinner party. It is vulgar to frown upon the habit as if it were an indicator of infidelity (in the masturbator) or inadequacy (in the abstainer). Masturbation has sundry roles in a relationship, prime among them keeping you in touch with the ebb and flow of your body's sexual preferences—and those of your partner, too. In addition, it is a refreshing (and nonfattening) study break, it offers stress relief, it tones your libido, it tones your pelvic-floor muscles (which can improve your Os), it is STD-proof, it requires no cuddling, and it puts a smile on your face. When practiced as a couple, it can serve as foreplay or sex, it allows you to demonstrate your patented moves to each other, and it is your best hope for simultaneous orgasms (though gentleman and ladies know that this spectacle is overrated). Lovers would do well to masturbate together as practice for phone sex—if one or both parties is shy, they might practice while watching a salacious film together, or perhaps just with the lights dimmed.

It is erroneous to consider one's libido something to be called on with reserve, as if it were an ungracious host and too many visits would outwear one's welcome. On the contrary, most ladies and gentlemen find that the more they call upon their libido while alone, the more they wish to call upon it with a partner. Our libidos, for the most part, are extroverts: energized when brought out to play, dulled when ignored. So be lightsome in your masturbatory habits, dear friends, for studies have shown it can only improve your sex lives.

Of course, your partners will not always be thusly enlightened, and it may be required that you explain your masturbatory ways. So long as you do not choose solo sex over congress, you are beyond reproof, though it is gracious to reassure your partner that he or she need not envy your relationship with your right hand (or the corner of the coffee table). Perhaps they find the act objectionable because they view it as a second-rate substitute for sex—in which case, your onanism might feel like a betrayal to them. Or perhaps they view it as a portal to cheating—especially if you are wont to do it to porn. It is mannerly to explain that you frequently think of your partner while serving yourself, that the act simply tides you over till you can look upon their face again. It would not be unseemly to employ a physiological argument—sometimes it is no more than a need for tension release, what is called a "maintenance orgasm" in some circles.

Once you have made your point—and made it clear that you do not intend to forfeit the habit—there is no need to be a braggart about it. It is not necessary to sneak around or lie, of course, but it would be indecorous to grab your favorite skin mag and head to the bathroom, hollering "See you in ten minutes, honey!" The gentleman or lady practices discretion—save your trashiest porn for sessions when there is no chance your partner will walk in on you, and avoid rubbing one out in the living room when you are expecting your partner over for dinner.

> The gentleman or lady never filches their
> partner's thirty-dollar-a-jar face lotion/hair
> product/extra virgin olive oil for self-service
> without asking, albeit delicately, first.

The Peanut Gallery:
How to Remain a Gracious Friend

No well-bred man or woman would expect a partner to relinquish a best
friend for the sake of a long-term relationship. The habit of abandoning
one's bosom buddies for a hot ticket is intolerable. It would be ignorant,
however, to pretend that one's friendships will remain unaltered by the
arrival of a significant other—if we apply logic to the situation, one simply has less time. Additionally, when you find yourself suddenly yoked,
your friends may lament the loss of spontaneity. No longer can they call
you after midnight on a Friday night and expect you to meet them at the
7-Eleven for a Super Big Gulp. For if you are not already out with them,
then in all likelihood you are snuggling in front of a roaring fire (or perchance a television) with your sweet one. Loyal friends do not chide the
newly yoked simply because a little advance notice is necessary for them
to come out and play—nor does the yoked one pout when they are not
called on for these spontaneous outings. A lady of our acquaintance who
did not wish to sacrifice spontaneity for couplehood *planned* for it; she
informed her young steed that Mondays and Wednesdays were her "see
what comes up" evenings—evenings when she would not see him, even if
she had no plans, evenings when she would be around after midnight for
spontaneous outings to the 7-Eleven. However, most ladies and gentlemen may find this approach a tad overwrought, and may prefer simply to
invest in a datebook. Umpteen other complications may present themselves: you find your partner's friends insipid; your partner finds your
buddies' favorite dive bar coarse and rank; you cannot bear the company
of your best friend's lover, et cetera. The following points of etiquette

should ensure your friends are there to pick up the pieces if and when that exquisite creature (whose company you are tempted to sacrifice so much for) tramples all over your heart.

- It is gauche to expect one's lover to give up Ladies' Poker Tuesdays/ Gentlemen's Watercolor Wednesdays.
- It is outmoded to take for granted that Saturday night is a date night. However, only the vulgar lady or gentleman plans a no-dates-allowed bar crawl every Saturday of the month.
- A gentleman or lady always honors the first plans made, whether with a friend or a partner.
- The "third wheel" is a social construct and civilized gentlemen and ladies pay it no heed. They do not find it weird to socialize as a group of three simply because two of the three will be having sexual relations later that night. However, the two who are rutting should be sensitive to any lingering feelings of discomfort the third party may be feeling, and should avoid engaging in passion-ate efforts that would frighten the horses.
- It is churlish to abandon one's friends of the fairer sex (whichever sex one finds fairest) because one's partner is jealous or finds the friendship inappropriate. However, the refined lady or gentleman might wish to tone down their typical flirtatious behavior around these friends if it makes their partner uncomfortable—especially early in a relationship, when insecurities might be rampant. Pla-tonic ass-grabbing, in particular, should be put on hold.
- When socializing without their partners, gentlemen and ladies should avoid the odious habit of treating single people of the fairer sex (again, whichever sex they consider fairest) as the enemy. Do not emulate a married gentleman of our acquaintance who refuses to engage in even polite chatter with unattached ladies—as if infidelity were a contagious disease and the single people who walk among us carry the strain.

No matter how deeply in love you find yourself, your best friend nevertheless deserves your confidence. If he or she tells you, "Please don't tell a soul," they do not mean, "Please don't tell a soul excepting of course your girlfriend/boyfriend."

A gentleman or lady never assumes a date is welcome when socializing with one or two intimate friends—it is polite to ask if one's partner may join the festivities. For larger gatherings, this is an unnecessary formality.

Regarding Your Partner's Friends

The gentleman or lady does not judge a partner's friends as quickly as they would judge a stranger. It is correct to assume that the people in a partner's social circle (and in particular their closest friends) are upstanding citizens worthy of respect until proved otherwise. In fact, we would all do well to act as if this were so more often in the world at large, though for now these two advice ladies shall dream a little smaller. To grant one's partner's friends a second, third, even fifth chance at a first impression is a class badge that distinguishes true ladies and gentlemen from plebeians. The gentleman or lady who finds their partner's friend unbearable does not question their partner's taste, but rather seeks to discover the fabric from which the friendship is rendered. Ask not, "What on earth do you see in that mooncalf?" but rather, "I feel as if I do not know Mr. Smith as well as I ought; tell me more about him." The gentleman or lady never suggests that the friend be discarded. And it is the height of vulgarity to openly sulk or insult when in the company of this friend. It is perfectly correct, however, to request that your partner see this friend on their own time—assuming that the aforementioned discreet line of questioning has failed to warm your heart toward them.

Regarding Your Friends' Partners

It is unnecessary to add that none but plebeians would refuse to give their friends' partners the aforementioned second, third, or fifth chances. You would do well to remember the affright such meetings can cause, and the odd effect this can have on a personality—it is therefore only polite to favor your friend's impression over your own, at least for the first month or two. The lady or gentleman is careful to judge a friend's significant other based on that friend's apparent happiness, more so than on how much "fun" the significant other is to be around.

That said, to be subjected five nights a week to a friend's slow-witted and uptight significant other is insufferably dull. After a few months it is acceptable to at least form an opinion on their "fun factor." So what is a lady or gentleman to do when a friend's main squeeze comes up short? You may not be so forthright as to *tell* your friend you would rather stay home and crochet than be forced to explain another witticism to their sweetheart, though it is not required that you become best buddies. While it is inelegant to exclude the dunderhead from major social events, it is not necessary to join their book club or double-date every Friday. You must always treat them with deference, but you would be wise to ensure the encounters take place in large, group settings, where the amount of deference you are required to summon is minimal.

If, however, you object to a friend's significant other for reasons having to do with *their* happiness, then it is prudent to share this opinion. Again, the civilized lady or gentleman always waits several weeks before coming to this conclusion. But once you become *convinced* this person is not fit for your friend, is not treating your friend as they ought, or is misleading or abusing your friend in some manner—then you may not hold your tongue. It is your obligation, as a friend, to speak up. And you would do well to speak up the moment you become convinced, lest you find yourself at their wedding, forced to break the silence echoing through the hall of the chapel after the minister has commanded, "If anyone here today knows of any just reason why these two people should not be married, speak now or forever hold your peace." Remember, however, that to make such a pronouncement is extreme behavior, liable to rock the very foundation of a friendship (though only temporarily, one would hope). It is thus advisable to be 100 percent sure your bias is grounded in true concern, and not simply your inability to relate to your friend's beau.

Finally, when you do confess your misgivings, do not do so with a flourish, as though pulling back a curtain concealing the Wizard of Oz. Speak graciously and with tact, and then listen as your friend responds. Avoid making an ultimatum or staging an intervention unless your friend is in true danger—if it is simply their heart on the line, then all you may do is give fair warning and withdraw to the sidelines, where you should wait with a pint of ice cream for the inevitable crash and burn. (See The Rules of Disengagement on p. 168 for more on how to handle the crash and burn.)

 ## OPEN RELATIONSHIPS

There are no laws of love. There are, however, traditions. And should you find yourself in a fairly traditional relationship—that is, a monogamous one—then everyone from Shakespeare to Jerry Springer will tell you what you can and cannot expect from said relationship. However, if you resolve to throw tradition to the wind and attempt one of these new-fangled open relationships, you may find yourself flailing. It need not be as troublesome as it sounds—in fact, were we all forced to be so open about our intentions, etiquette guides like this one would be mostly moot.

It is not vulgar to want to see more than one person at a time. It is not vulgar to have no desire for monogamy, whether you are twenty-two or fifty-two. It is not vulgar to *never* desire monogamy. But it *is* unspeakably vulgar to pretend that monogamy is what you want in order to procure something else. In an open relationship, open communication comes before all else. You are obliged to be diligent in defining the terms and boundaries of your romantic situation. "Open" does not indicate a lack of rules, but rather that you write—and follow—the rules yourselves. The points of consideration below should be deliberated and agreed upon. There is no correct or incorrect answer to each question, it is simply required that, were the two of you to be asked these questions on the Newly-Wed Game, you would each give the same answer:

How will you redefine physical fidelity? Is it anything goes? Or just oral, just anal, just making out? What about acts that are tradi-tionally viewed as more romantic, such as hand-holding, eye-contact, pillow talk?

How will you redefine emotional fidelity? How do you feel about extra-curricular *romantic* entanglements? Can you go on dates with someone other than your main squeeze, or should it be naught but fucking? Will you be permitted to have regular booty calls, or would you prefer one-night stands only?

How much information will you each require? Will you each ask permission each time (a phone call to their mobile, for example)? Would you like to meet your partner's bit on the side, or just hear the sordid details the next morning? Is it acceptable to attempt a pickup while out with your partner? Will you, perchance, be each other's wing man or woman? Or would you rather know nothing at all?

Will you bond as a group? Are the two of you interested in swing-ing, play parties, threeways, or more? (If so, see the Casual Sex chapter on p. 75.) Or are you solely interested in one-on-one activities?

Is it different for ladies? Or gentlemen? Do slightly different rules apply if your bit on the side is of a gender other than your partner's?

May you hunt it down? Is it acceptable to seek out opportunities (for example, by posting a personal) or should you just take it as it comes (pardon the pun)? Or is it only acceptable if you are out of town? If your partner is away on business, will you be allowed to have an overnight guest? Are overnight guests in hotel rooms permissible? Or will you be expected to always depart before sunup?

〜➡ **Is your open relationship in the public domain?** Are you comfortable having friends know the status of your relationship? What about coworkers? Family members?

 There is only one universal law by which all open-relationship participants must abide: No booty on the side shall be procured under false pretenses. In other words, every fling deserves to be apprised of your relationship status, in case they should prefer not to be an accessory to such a modern arrangement.

Typecasting

The open relationship is not for everyone. It is an incredibly new sociological phenomenon—it has yet to be fully studied or completely understood. In fact, many people fail to believe it even exists. It is a discrete segment of the population that boasts the neurotransmitter capable of successfully blocking such age-old human emotions as jealousy, insecurity, and possessiveness—a requirement for the success of such lifestyles.

Just as there are early birds and night owls, smokers and nonsmokers, cat people and dog people, so there are monogamists and polyamorists. Interestingly, not everyone is true to their true selves. Plenty of people suffer what they consider the indignity of an open relationship because they believe their partner has monogamy potential ("My love will change them"), while others force themselves into the monogamy mold because they think it is the only elegant thing to do—and these people are all wretched.

It is ignorant to think that these groups are divided along gender lines—ladies and gentlemen alike find contentment in open relation-ships, just as they do in monogamous ones. And it is inelegant to pass judgment either way. Nor should you have to choose one or the other and be resolute in that decision—discovering which model suits you best in-volves sampling the options. It is not gauche to attempt to condition yourself to enjoy the benefits of polyamory (forsooth, there are some). Of course, then you risk losing the benefits of monogamy (forsooth, there are many). It is only required that you make this decision for yourself—and not for a lover, whether current or potential.

On a final note, we must find fault with those people who claim monogamy is bourgeois, no more than a socially conditioned desire. How is one to separate social constructs from one's heart's desire and one's genetic coding? And who is to say what is proper or improper? An army of leather-clad gimps frowning on monogamy is no less bullheaded than a Congress full of suits pushing family values. In fact, bridging the gap be-tween those two extremes is what makes sex sublime: Kink can spice up monogamy and monogamy can make kink—especially power play—even more intense. Some of us play well with others, and some of us do better with just one playmate. There is no shame in wanting one person, and one person alone, to tie you to the bedpost and drip hot wax on your nipples for as long as you both shall live.

THE RULES OF DISENGAGEMENT

When people break up, there is usually so much sad-ness, pain, and red-faced, vein-popping hatred brew-ing that decorum takes a back seat to bad behavior and insults about

sexual-skill level. ("You're breaking up with me? Good luck finding someone who'll fall for a limp dick like you!"—more commonly known as the "I
got your best years" rebuttal.) But if both parties would simply take a moment to collect their thoughts, to breathe from the abdomen as if in yoga
class, to realize that there cannot be that much hate without a little leftover love, then parting ways could actually become a more civilized
process. Or perhaps not. But at least it could become just another mildly
unpleasant fact of life. Feelings could be spared and some dignity saved.
If you can manage to follow the rules of disengagement when it comes to
breaking hearts and heartbreak, you are truly an exemplary citizen.

Rules for the Dumper

Dumping is a delicate art. The onus is mostly on you to do the right thing:
You are responsible for your soon-to-be ex's care throughout the entire
dumping process; you are not allowed to disengage emotionally once you
have decided it is over, no matter how irrationally they seem to take the
bad news. You must take pains to ensure their well-being: *Plan* the dumping, do it deliberately but thoughtfully, kill them with kindness. This is not
the time for brutal honesty: No "I've never loved you" or "I met this total
hottie the other night and I'd like to pursue a future with them in it." In
fact, this is one of the few times when little white lies are permissible, as
long as you remain convinced it will make things easier on your partner—
rather than easier on your wussy ass (see Sidebar on p. 171).

Of course, all of the above bets are off if you are doing the dumping
because you discovered your partner cheated on you. In that case, fuck
decorum.

So how should a lady or gentleman approach the dumping? Let us begin with how *not* to approach it. If you have been courting for longer than
two weeks or you have had congress more than three times (and it was
not expressly casual congress, see p. 75), then it is unspeakably rude to
do it over email or via text messaging. If you have been courting for

longer than two months or you have had congress more than, let us say, twenty times, then you may not do it over the phone. You may not do it in a bar unless you are both truly soused and neither of you will recall it in the morning. It is uncharitable to do it immediately after your partner has successfully kicked a stress-relieving foul habit, such as biting their nails or smoking crack. You may not do it at their favorite bar, restaurant, or park—that is sacred space they will need to take refuge in after you dump them. You may not do it in any place that might taint an otherwise beautiful memory the two of you previously shared, lest the dumping overshadow the BM (that is Beautiful Memory, though we suppose it becomes the more traditional BM if you break up with them there also). Do not do it before the lunch hour; later in the day is preferable, otherwise they will be forced to endure a full five or six hours before the drinking with a good friend commences (or a self-imposed guilt trip for drinking before noon). Do not do it over dinner—this simply prolongs the inevitable and leaves the dumpee with the impression that they were as pitiable and laughable as a rat dining on cheese in a trap. If some straw happens to break the camel's back while you are out to dinner and you decide you simply can go on no longer, then it is polite to at least wait until the entrées have been cleared to avoid embarrassing the waitstaff or wasting a good meal.

When you meet up to break the news, it is vulgar to dally around the subject. Small talk will not be appreciated—your beau will see straight through your chitchat charade. The gentleman or lady always avoids cliches. "I love you, but I'm not in love with you" is so overdone, one might as well send a candygram to do the deed. Even though you may desire never to lay eyes on this creature again, they still deserve talk from the heart, not the cheese factory. If you can muster tears (*naturally*, not by pulling on a nose or pubic hair), that is always a nice personal touch. Do not expect and certainly do *not* initiate breakup sex. If the dumpee initiates, you must 1) resist ever so slightly, and 2) then be absolutely, totally convinced that the dumpee is doing it, at least in part, for themselves (that is, they are more interested in making you *regret* your decision than in attempting to change your mind).

Regarding the aftermath: Do not be so ostentatious as to post an online personal for at least three weeks: A friend of a friend of your ex's *will* see it and it *will* get back to your ex. If you should encounter the dumpee's friend in a social setting later that night/week/month, it is appropriate to act sad and/or contrite. In fact, should you live in a small town, you would be wise to instead stay home for a few days and entertain your friends there. There is no rule of etiquette mandating how long you should wait for a post-breakup shag with someone else, *so long as* you are absolutely, positively sure there is *no way* your ex will ever discover you, and so long as you are absolutely, positively sure you will *not* be reconciling with the ex. To break up with a partner in order to have sex with someone else only to get back together once the deed is done is not just bad form, it is grounds for a first-class ticket to hell. And in hell, there are no manners. Finally, it should be unnecessary to add that screwing or wooing any friends, coworkers, or family members of the dumpee is completely unacceptable for at least two years. However, a true class act would abide by an eternal hands-off policy when it comes to those people.

Lies That Are Allowed

- Why you are dumping them: Provide a soft version of the truth.
- How hard this decision was for you: It is always "very hard." But avoid being too melodramatic by saying it is one of the hardest or *the* hardest thing you have ever had to do—that sounds not only insincere, but also condescending.
- What you really think about their parents/their most annoying habit/that body part they are so insecure about: Lies, damn lies!
- What you are doing right after finishing dumping them: Lie, unless you really are going home to sob into your pillow for ten days.
- If there is anybody else: It depends. If there is someone else you would like to pursue, but you have not yet had relations with this person, do not tell; if there is someone else with whom you have committed adultery, but whom you do not intend to see again (i.e., the fling was simply a catalyst), do not tell; if there is someone you have already begun seeing and you intend to continue to do so, *do tell*.

Rules for the Dumpee

One of the only agreeable aspects to being dumped is the temporary freedom it allows you to chuck most civilized behavior out the window. This does not mean you become a total boor—remember, a little bit of shame is what separates us from the animals. And you certainly do not want to give your dumper any more reasons to believe they made the right decision in leaving you.

When you realize you are being cut off, remain calm. Listen to what your now-ex has to say. Neither pick up heavy objects nor threaten to throw them. No screaming, ladies and gentlemen—that vulgar behavior is for babies and Shannon Doherty alone. You may cry, of course. And it is perfectly acceptable to excuse yourself to the bathroom to splash water on your face, blow your nose, throw up, punch out the tampon/condom dispenser, et cetera. Be sure to return with a few tissues: A river of snot flowing from your nose will only make this process harder on you (and easier on your dumper).

"Why?" is a legitimate question—but you must accept the first . . . okay, the second answer. "Is there anyone else?" is also acceptable. Asking them to reconsider, however, is strongly ill-advised. You may ask them to stay over, "just one more night," but only if you are capable of polite behavior the following morn-

Sleeping with the Enemy— Booty-Calling an Ex

- The dumpee must be the initiator for the first two times. After that, it is considered polite for the dumper to initiate so the dumpee does not feel doubly pathetic.
- You do not discuss "what went wrong."
- You do not discuss "why aren't we still together."
- You *do* discuss how great you used to be in bed together.
- Ladies first, no matter who dumped whom.
- Facials, rough sex, bondage, water sports, and/or doggie style may help provide "closure," assuming all parties grant permission and the person who got screwed over in the relationship is the one with the power in *this* screwing situation.

(See p. 82 for more on booty-call etiquette.)

ing, and will not proceed to blame them for using you and/or leading you on.

Permissible behavior during the immediate recovery period includes: Getting sloppy-drunk to the point of passing out, eating food straight out of the container, not showering or changing your underwear, adopting a rather indelicate nickname for your ex, trash-talking your ex to your best friend. The above uncouth behavior should not exceed seven days.

The rebound fuck is perfectly acceptable. And unlike the dumper, you are exceedingly less constrained in terms of suitable partners. Best friends and family members of your ex are still offlimits. However, their

What No Ex Deserves

The following gaucheries are unforgivable in *any* breakup situation, no matter how wrenching: Posting naked (and/or unflattering) pictures of your ex on the Internet; Jeopardizing their job (by dropping anonymous tips to their boss about their after-hours abuse of the office photocopier); Announcing their deepest, darkest secret to a roomful of mutual friends; Reporting their recent tax evasion to the IRS; Reporting them to the INS for deportation. No matter how awful the ex, you, as a civilized human being, should not stoop to made-for-TV revenge tactics. Have faith in karma, dear friends— the evil ex *will* get what is coming to them in the end.

acquaintances and coworkers (the boss excluded) are acceptable therapy fucks. And you need not take extra pains to be discreet—it is inelegant to take out an ad in *The New York Times* announcing your every new lay, but worry not if it should somehow get back to your ex via the rumor mill. Of course, the usual rules of engagement apply to every rebound. No misleading, dishonest, or destructive sex. In fact, your surrogate should be at least vaguely aware that this will probably be nothing more than a palate-cleansing hookup for you. See the Casual Sex chapter for the finer points of etiquette in these situations.

Finally, you may not under any circumstances, save for hospitalization, call your ex (especially when you are drunk) to "just talk" within the first six weeks of a breakup. You may not tell them how much you miss them and how deeply you desire to get back together, and you may not shame them into considering reconciliation with complaints of depression, phantom pregnancy scares, and/or empty threats of suicide. Call your therapist instead. Once this six-week grace period has passed, you may request a "Closure Meeting," but only if your best friend believes you are mentally prepared to handle it. (See Post-Breakup Rules for Everyone on p. 175.)

Rules for the Best Friend

A good friend instinctually knows they serve an important role during this time. And a well-mannered friend accepts this responsibility without hesitation or complaint. You must put all your problems on hold temporarily and dedicate your time and attention to humoring the dumper/dumpee's self-pity festival.

When the trash talk commences, simply nod your head and agree with your friend. Never express any sentiment of your *own* about the ex that might compromise your position, now or later—your friend may still harbor feelings for the ex and feel protective of them, or worse, may end up back together with said ex. A lady of our acquaintance broke up with a gentleman no less than six times before she admitted he was her One True Love—had her friends joined her in the vitriolic rebuke of him that accompanied each breakup, they would have had many hats to eat. It is therefore advisable to wait at least several months (or until the last ember of possible reconciliation has been extinguished) before expressing your own unique happiness over the separation. It is, however, acceptable to refer to the ex by the new derogatory and indelicate term your friend has assigned them. At no point should you say, "I told you so." Never mention the time their ex got drunk and hit on you. Do, however, remind them of the time their ex did something fairly benign but extremely embarrassing, such as fall for an Internet pyramid scheme, or something *temporarily* unflattering, such as that one haircut you secretly referred to as "the toilet plunger."

And yes, gentle readers, as the best friend, it is in extremely bad taste to make your own play for the ex (or to encourage their play for you)— now or *ever*. (See Exes Etiquette on p. 177 for what to do if you just cannot fight the feeling.)

Post-Breakup Rules for Everyone

Regarding material items, a gentleman or lady is never petty. It is correct to return all personal items you know they desire, but may be too polite or proud to ask for. Just because you are broken up and may no longer respect your ex, it is nevertheless unspeakably vulgar to publicly screen any off-color pictures or videos you may have taken of them. In fact, a true gentleman or lady will return all compromising materials (including negatives) to the ex in question. Joint custody of pets simply does not work—do not make your Chihuahua reenact *Kramer vs. Kramer*. If in doubt, anything warm, fuzzy, and comforting should remain with the dumpee. Anything scaly or aquatic may be decided by a coin toss. The schedule of working out the details of these exchanges is to be determined by the dumpee—should the dumpee insist on settling all affairs immediately, then the dumper must oblige; should the dumpee fail to bring it up, then the dumper waits at least ten days before requesting his or her favorite T-shirt (the one that smells like Snuggle fabric softener).

It is inadvisable to destroy any items of sentimental value in the immediate aftermath of a breakup. You would do well to wait a few weeks until your head has cleared. You *may* put those items in storage immediately; however, the considerate dumper always leaves a few items as they were—a photo on a desk or a fridge—should there be a chance the dumpee will see them in the next few weeks (when stopping by the apartment to drop something off, for example).

A "closure meeting" is also the dumpee's prerogative. In short, the dumpee has the right in all cases to be friendly or distant. Dumpees have not many rights; let us gracefully concede the few they possess. The dumper must oblige the dumpee's request for one closure meeting anywhere from six weeks to nine months after the breakup. If after nine months no wrap-up meeting has been requested, the dumper may safely assume that closure was not necessary. Depending on the length of the relationship and the circumstances of the breakup, more than one closure session may be necessary to cover all items on the agenda; more than three, however, is excessive. Assuming that the dumpee follows etiquette and requests the meeting at least six weeks after the breakup, the dumper should expect to be slightly less soft with the "why I dumped you" truth. However, all other points of etiquette should be followed to the letter. It is not officially considered a "closure meeting" if it ends in sex (for exceptions, see the Sleeping with the Enemy sidebar, p. 172), though mild fondling or Frenching is acceptable.

The Freedom of Information Act

- The dumpee may announce in public "It was mutual," even if they got dropped harder than a sack of bricks.
- The dumpee may *not* announce in public "I did the dumping," or "They cheated on me" if that is not the truth.
- The dumpee is free to disparage their ex's bedroom skills, but only to very close friends; the *dumper* is free to do so only if the dumpee breaks any of the rules of disengagement herein.
- Neither party may log on to the other's email account, even if it is simply to confirm the ex is abiding by all rules of disengagement. "They were asking for it by cheating on me/dumping me/never going down on me/not changing their password" are not acceptable excuses. The dumper in particular is advised to change all passwords, just in case.
- Neither party should compromise mutual friends by pumping them for information on the ex's activities.
- The gentleman or lady does not go on a fact-finding mission about their ex's new life until he or she is ready to handle said facts in a mature, sophisticated fashion. The dumpee always garners a second opinion (usually from a best friend) as to whether they can handle the truth.

(For more on Exes Etiquette, see p. 177.)

There are several points of etiquette to bear in mind once you begin to court others. There is a difference between a favorite movie or song of yours and a movie or song that you and your ex used to modify with "our." The former are fine to share with new partners; the latter should not be shared with anyone else for at least five years out of respect for the dead relationship. Every partner deserves a fresh sex toy; there should be no sloppy seconds when it comes to dildos and butt plugs (see Sharing Toys on p. 122). It is acceptable, however, to finish half-used tubes of lube, either alone or with others. You may wear lingerie and sleepwear bought for you by an ex in front of new partners, so long as you did not lose your virginity or spend your honeymoon in it. The lady or gentlemen never has sex while listening to a mix made by an ex. (For more information on the etiquette of meeting and greeting an ex, see Exes Etiquette, below.)

EXES ETIQUETTE

Just as defending the fifth amendment is most exacting when the free speech in question is truly horrible to one's ears, so the upkeep of manners is most taxing in the company of an odious (or worse, odious and yet still ravishing) ex. In cases such as these, prudence advises us to consider etiquette our best chance at saving face, at maintaining at least a modicum of pride. So the ex stole your smile, your happiness, your cat? Do not then let them abscond with your manners, too!

Let Us Be Friends

It is beyond our jurisdiction to determine whether you should forge a friendship with your ex. That is an individual decision fraught with messy emotions (and occasionally, messy sex acts) too numerous to mention. Some ladies and gentlemen are friends with every person they have so much as laid lips on, while others prefer to close the book on a relationship that has run its course. Neither approach is necessarily more elegant; rather, it is how you handle the situation that determines your character.

Ladies and gentlemen should never lose their dignity when conversing with an ex—assuming that the two of you have moved beyond the afore-mentioned official closure stage. If there was any chance that you were likely to break down, to throw heavy objects, to throw yourself at their knees, or in any other way to take the encounter with ill temper, you had far better entrust your interactions to the pen or keyboard—or perhaps, more wisely, to the annals of relationship history.

If you are confident you can handle the friendship with aplomb, you would do well to set boundaries. How much information about your ex's new life do you require? As with an open relationship, this is simply a matter of striking a balance you are both comfortable with. Prudence advises you never to ask a question if you surmise the answer will distress you. In addition, you may wish to redraw boundaries depending on your current relationship status—while you may enjoy the occasional stumble down memory lane after a six-hour pub crawl with your ex, that is not necessarily the done thing when one is in a long-term relationship. And while we admire the maturity of those ladies and gentlemen who are ca-pable of maintaining easy friendships with their exes, we do look suspi-ciously upon those persons who feel it necessary to touch base with those exes on a daily basis.

Allow Me to Introduce You to My New Fuck Puppet: Greeting Exes in Public

Whether you are friends with your exes or prefer to look upon them only in voodoo-doll form, there may come a time when you encounter an ex in public, and one—or both—of you is with a date. It is unnecessary and stilted to give either the ex or the current a title when making the intro-ductions; do not say, "This is my girlfriend/this *was* my girlfriend"—no

> **Bringing new partners to a place you know your ex frequents is an amusement altogether to be condemned.**

doubt that will be apparent to all parties by the awkwardness of your tone or the twitch in your left eye. A simple name exchange is enough before making a polite but swift exit. It is always unacceptable to abandon one's date to offer solace to an ex in distress—you must wait until the conclusion of your date before making a comfort call. Remember, dear readers, tact produces good manners. Do not engage your ex and your current in a lengthy discussion on the many varied uses of baking soda, simply to have balance and harmony in your life, if it is clear the conversation is excruciating to the other two participants. Finally, when encountering an ex whose heart you stomped all over, congratulations on their newfound happiness/relationship/bisexual identity can sometimes be too fervidly expressed. To act thusly is rather to suggest that he or she has been successful against great odds.

Ex Talk

Gentlemen and ladies are earnestly advised that new partners rarely wish to hear about old flames. Anything like bragging or wallowing should not be indulged in—and even trash-talking your ex gives you the air of an uncaring lout. However, you would be a fool to pretend we

---

Dingdong, the Witch Is at the Front Door

Encounters with old flames reach the height of embarrassment when an ex drops by unannounced while you are entertaining for two—especially if the butler is not available to announce "Madame is not at home." It is for  this reason we must strongly recommend that you *never* stop by an ex's abode unannounced. Should your own ex be unversed in this point of etiquette, you should be honest—but not too honest. It is correct to say, "My friend and I were about to sit down to dinner, may I give you a call later?" It is not correct to say, "My foxy new playmate was about to do me up the butt with a strap-on, may I give you a call later?"

had no prior dating record. In fact, a completely blank dating slate would give us pause. The following tips should ensure that when the subject of exes finds its way into your conversation with a new partner, you handle it with decorum.

- It cannot be too strongly insisted upon that you not discuss your exes' performance in the bedroom—even, or perhaps especially, if it is to disparage them.
- Prudence advises you to inquire as to your partners' preexisting sexual preferences in only the most *general* terms. For example, ask "What would you like me to do with my tongue?" and not "What was your asshole ex-boyfriend like in bed? I have a bigger dick, right?"
- Similarly, it is a breach of etiquette to draw comparisons between exes and your current partner, no matter how favorable. Ladies and gentlemen know that past loves and current ones are apples and oranges, and should not be compared, lest you give the impression of fancying a banana in another fortnight.
- Even the most refined of ladies and gentlemen have made the unseemly mistake of asking a new partner, "Remember that time we . . . ?" when they were, in fact, remembering another significant other. To attempt to ignore the mistake—or worse, to badger the new partner into "remembering" the incident to cover one's arse—is lame. Additionally, it is uncouth to prolong the awkwardness by explaining "anyone could have made that mistake." The lady or gentleman who makes such a mistake is particular to be more selfless than usual in the bedroom later that day.
- Photographs of exes should never decorate one's quarters. In fact, it is only acceptable to show a partner photographs of one's ex if one or both of your hairstyles looks suitably retro (i.e., hideous) in the image.

Dating the Floor Model

It is offending against good taste as well as against common sense to woo a friend's ex. But sometimes, gentle readers, Cupid deigns to shoot an arrow through the heart of good taste and common sense. It is not hard to understand how this attraction happens—especially if your friend has good taste in both friends and lovers—though it is immeasurably hard to determine whether pursuing it is worth the risk to the friendship. In all cases, one must wait until at least six months have passed (or closure has been reached, whichever takes longer), no matter how brief the initial relationship. If it is worth breaking protocol for, then it is worth waiting half a year for. As with dating a friend's relative (see p. 11), it is necessary to first announce your intentions to your friend, though you should not ask *permission* if you are not prepared to accept a "mais non!" Next, though we would not be so presumptuous as to speak on Cupid's behalf, we would venture that even that little munchkin would not be so mischievous as to cause you to fall for the jackhole who put your very best friend's heart through the blender late last autumn. In such a case, we would strongly advise you to wait out the crush at least a year and do everything in your power to avoid said ex. Be wary, gentle readers, of mistaking a starcrossed notion that your union is "impossible!" for true love. If you decide to proceed, we cannot, in good faith, give you any advice lest we give the impression of condoning such behavior. Finally, it is usually acceptable to date a friend's former booty call—one has agreeable insight into matters of salacity, but emotionally, the model should barely be worn.

CHAPTER VI
The Unmentionables

The issues we shall cover in this chapter are not for the faint of heart. While they should never be discussed in polite company—at the dinner table, during a family reunion, while taking tea with the Queen—they nevertheless require delicate and polite negotiation when they arise. Before you protest, we would submit that to take easy offense at the facts of life and of flesh is to betray a pitiable rigidity of ideas regarding what is normal and natural. Yes, dear reader, queefs and farts happen. Do get over it. Labia come in all shapes and sizes and colors. Please accept it. If you have sex during menses, things are going to take on a red hue. We ask that you cultivate a sense of humor and try broadening your horizons a bit, as any thoroughbred citizen should.

 ## "IMPOLITE" EMISSIONS

Body Odor

As Henry David Thoreau said, "There is no odor so bad as that which rises from goodness tainted." You may be the picture of politeness, but if you are remiss in your duties as a member of civilization to keep yourself clean and relatively sweet smelling, you may as well eat with your hands, scratch your posterior in public, and play with your feces—for you are nothing but an animal.

As we touched upon in the Kissing section of the Courting chapter (p. 29), ladies and gentlemen should take care to keep their breath fresh, whether by not smoking, avoiding coffee, brushing their teeth and tongue often, and/or carrying breath mints on their person at all times. Gum should be avoided whenever possible: cows chew cud, civilized ladies and gentlemen do not. If there is no other alternative and your breath could wipe out an entire village of black ants with one blow, then you may deposit a piece of gum into your mouth. However, you must be sure to chew quietly with your mouth closed, for there is nothing so inelegant as a gum smacker. We will not even speak of the lowly sorts who blow and pop bubbles. Whether you employ mints or gum, those around you should not be able to discern in any way that you have something in your mouth; the only giveaway should be the sweet scent emanating from your pie hole. Always carry enough to offer to your date or others around you. If you are on a date and only have one piece left, you must refrain from partaking if you are unable to split it in half.

In days of old, smoking was considered quite an elegant affair: after-dinner cigars and long, silver cigarette holders were de rigueur. These days, it is less fashionable—indulged in mostly by addicts, rebellious teenagers, young college maids who believe it makes them "look cool," and rock stars both real and imagined. If you, too, find yourself stuck on the end of a death stick, you must concede to the preferences of those around you—at least those in your immediate vicinity. Do not speak of inalienable rights, for stinking up the air as if you were impersonating Pig Pen is the ultimate imposition, an odiferous invasion of personal space. Instead, take your fixes when you can get them, but be at the ready to give them up when courtesy calls for it. If you find yourself in the presence of a nonsmoker, it is polite to ask if they would mind if you lit up. Honor every negative answer. If they are so gracious as to allow you your filthy habit, be careful to blow the smoke away from all of them, taking into consideration the wind and ventilation of your surroundings, for nothing is so offensive as a cloud of toxic fumes blown straight into one's visage.

If you are a committed smoker, we highly recommend wooing fellow smokers. When foolishly disregarding our advice and dating a nonsmoker, you must never assume you may light up in their abode. Even if they give you permission, it is polite to always position yourself by an opened window, and to never smoke a post-coital cigarette in their bed. In fact, we recommend weaning yourself off this outmoded ritual lest you interrupt the precious cuddling time. If you simply cannot, we request again that you stick with your kind and date only fellow chimney stacks—there is little so repellant as a partner who climbs back in-between your freshly laundered sheets reeking like an overflowing ashtray. And never date a nonsmoker simply as incentive to quit; to do so is as self-serving as dating the boss's repugnant offspring to get a promotion. Should you fall for a lovely young smoke-free lass or lad and be struck with the desire to quit for them, you would do well to take your last puff *before* the first kiss.

As a nonsmoker, you may politely request that those in your company refrain from smoking if they are in your house, if you are eating, or if you are in bed (yours *or* theirs).

What if there be more delight in some perfumes than the breath with which your lover reeks? It is most unfortunate that those with halitosis rarely know they suffer from it. If you are on an early date, the most that good taste, as it were, allows you to do is offer up a mint. If you fear even that will cause offense, then delicately drop hints to influence fresh-breath behavior. For example, encourage them to skip the after-dinner coffee so you two can abscond to the promenade for a midnight walk under the moon, "before it gets too late." Unfortunately, their innocent ignorance of the situation may mean subtle hints will be lost on them. If this is the case, you must simply grin and bear it while taking shallow breaths. Prudence advises us to wait until after the fifth date, or after we have slept with the guilty party, to explicitly yet politely address the problem head on. "Darling, you know I absolutely adore you, but I must say . . ."

And so, it follows, if someone offers you a mint, do not be so quick to politely decline the offer, for it may not just be out of courtesy, but out of oxygen necessity, that they are extending the peppermint refreshment.

May we humbly suggest if you are vomiting the contents of your stomach into a porcelain bowl or a street gutter that you call the sex off? Not only is it rude to expect your date to kiss that mouth within twenty-four hours of such an emission, it is rude to subject them to your certain sexual shortcomings in such a state.

Perhaps one's offending odor is not limited to the mouth, but instead seems to ooze from every pore of one's being. It is the wise citizen who realizes BO ultimately emanates from within and conscientiously chooses to limit the number of toxins taken in. Certain foods and consumables can also affect the way you taste down below. The worst offenders, especially when it comes to your love juices (both men's and women's), are asparagus, coffee, booze, cigarettes, and some drugs (especially cocaine). Garlic and some Indian curry spices may be good for your health, but bad for your love life. You might also find that large quantities of broccoli, salty foods, alkaline-heavy foods like meats and fish, and dairy all make you taste a little off. Considerate ladies and gentlemen improve their flavor downtown as well as all over by eating melon, kiwi, pineapples, strawberries, and cinnamon. If you are a polite person, you will not request any oral attention after a night of overindulging in beer, hard liquor, coffee, cigarettes, or drugs. At the very least, you will first drink lots of water to flush out your system.

Perhaps you are a sweater. If so, be sure to shower once, if not twice daily, especially before sex, and consider shaving and using a natural deodorant, lest you frighten the horses. Keeping yourself clean via regular washings and fresh, breathable underwear will help prevent genital infections such as jock itch and yeast infections, which is the least you can do for yourself and your partners. It should be unnecessary to add that if you come down with such an infection, you must abstain from sex.

Let us say you find yourself falling in love, and the only obstacle to your complete bliss is an offensive scent produced from your partner's warm, moist places. Observe their daily habits so you can begin to gently suggest alternatives to their favorite Pakistani curry house, or request politely that they cut down on the cigarettes (at least for your sake), or propose the two of you shower together before getting into bed. You may only say something specific after you have gotten naked together at least three times, and only then when you can offer constructive criticism, in the most deferential matter, based on your observations.

However, it is excessively unbecoming to be aromatically prudish: A person's body parts are not supposed to smell like a summer's eve simply because a large corporation has deemed it so. Funky musk is a natural aphrodisiac. At least, it is when people's body chemistries are compatible. How your junction smells to one lover may not be how it smells to another; some may find it ranker than their driving instructor's BO, while others find it sweeter than the nectar of the gods; some might detect a hint of sour milk while others conjure mental images of lavender patches every time they take a breath. Above all, ladies and gentlemen should bear in mind that body odor is a very personal affair. You would do well to tread lightly when the topic is raised.

To douse oneself with perfume or cologne in place of a shower is as vulgar as sweeping dust under a rug. To douse oneself with perfume or cologne *after* a shower is as vulgar as hanging a vanilla car-freshener tree off a bouquet of freshly cut flowers.

Boogs

If you are prone to mucous build up, it is wise to carry a small pack of tissues on you for regular checkups. While the handkerchief still holds some appeal for those who long for the courteous traditions of yesteryear, truly modern ladies and gentlemen dismiss it as nothing more than a germ-riddled snot rag. Trimming nose hairs is a random act of kindness clandestinely extended toward everyone who may cast their gaze upon you throughout the day; fortuitously, it also helps prevent strays from creeping down into visible territory—another benefit for those in close communication (especially the ones who are shorter than you).

If you are on a date, no matter whether it is your first or your fiftieth, you are obligated to immediately let that person know if they have a dangling participle. Discretion and reserve are key: Simply say "You've got a little—" at which point you offer them a tissue or, if you have none, subtly run the back of your finger under your own nose two or three times. This is not an excuse to pick your own nose: think small, subtle motions. And you do *not* need to finish the sentence; if they are of quick wit, they will receive your meaning. Carry on the conversation as if nothing has happened. Do not make a fuss, point with your finger, or break out into hysterics, whether you are the informant or the victim. Mucous stalactites are only as dire as you make them. If the party you are with fails to follow this rule, simply shrug it off and persevere with your head held high (assuming you have ridden yourself of any nose trinkets). If you are in need of a tissue and your date does not offer you one, you may use the napkin in your lap.

If you are out of reach of any kind of cloth or paper receptacle for your boog, then and only then may you use your bare fingers—just be sure to wash your hands at the next available opportunity and keep them out of your mouth (*always* a civilized thing to do). If you are unsure whether or not you have taken care of the runaway, you may quietly ask your companion if it is gone, but you cannot lift your head up so they have full view of your brain. However, in these cases, it is preferable to excuse yourself and visit the mirror in the bathroom.

The same rules apply for food—most especially dark food—lodged in-between one's teeth. And no, silverware may not double as a makeshift toothpick.

> **The only correct final destination for the contents of your nasal cavity is a tissue—never the underside of the desk, behind your bed, or on the street. Our pens refuse to dignify the detestable "air hankies" with further discussion.**

Toots

When one is reasonably sure of ending up in bed with one's date later in the evening, there are measures one can take early on to avoid future flatulence. The biggest wind culprit is ingesting excess air, which happens when you chow down, when you do not chew, when you chew *gum* (yet another strike against gum chewing), when you smoke (as if it needed another strike), when you drink through a straw, and when you—say it is not so!—talk with your mouth full. None of which you should be doing on a first date, or in any kind of polite company. In addition, the following foods *may* make you toot even if you mash them into a pulp before swallowing: broccoli, cabbage, carrots, celery, raisins, prunes, onions, beans (all kinds), asparagus, pears, apples, peaches, whole grains, dairy, soda, and most especially Brussels sprouts. Of course, that does not leave much on the menu to work with. So as a general rule, we say eschew any dishes with beans, any dishes heavy on dairy, and any dishes served with Brussels sprouts.

While it is unhealthy to chronically hold in your gas, you must keep your butt cheeks clenched, if need be, during any early amorous exchanges. Remember, farting after sex is infinitely more agreeable than farting before it. Whether before or after, only the most offensive of barbarians make a spectacle of their digestive emissions with pull-my-finger jokes or Dutch ovens. Such childish things should be put away. However, when accidental emissions occur, it is similarly gauche to make a stink, as it were, about it. When this happens, you may either ignore it or laugh it off, depending on its volume and stench. Comic relief, in these cases, is encouraged: For example, the farter may say ironically, "I'm going to let that one slide, but don't do it again." It is best to simply consider such outbursts a fast-forward to greater intimacy.

Queefs

Ladies and gentlemen, vaginal "farts" occur naturally in this universe, and there is nothing you can do to prevent them. A queef is no more than the release of (nonodiferous) air from the vagina that was trapped during arousal or penetration. A lady's vagina expands when she is terribly excited, and so the air is usually expelled as penetrating objects shift, or as the vagina returns to its everyday state while you are cuddling. If you cannot ignore the queef (as most ladies and gentlemen are wont to do), but feel compelled to comment on it, speak of it as one would flatulence (as discussed above). To pull a face is terribly rude and insulting. If you are a chronic queefer and wish to disguise the habit, you might try cueing a sultry CD to serve as your sex-and-cuddle soundtrack.

Poo

We know of no greater romantic crisis then finding yourself on a date that is headed toward sex—indeed, when the sex is seemingly imminent—and you find yourself suddenly in need of taking a monster shit. To poo or not to poo, that is the question, dear readers.

First, you would do well to prevent such awkward situations with a preemptive strike via daily doses of fiber. Just a teaspoon of psyllium-husk powder stirred into your freshly squeezed morning orange juice will make you as regular as the changing of the guard, so you can plan your love-making accordingly.

But let us say the swordfish steak was tainted, and you now find your-self in the precarious position of having to drop the kids off at the pool in the middle of a date. If you are still out in public, at a restaurant or cocktail lounge, we suggest excusing yourself, retreating to the bath-room, and trying to take care of business. But you should do this only if you are confident it will take you less than five minutes to take care of said business, and there are no long lines. If the crowds are rowdy or you fear opening the floodgates will result in nothing less than a half an hour on the pot, you must abort. Do not be a daredevil or a martyr; feign a nondescript illness, express your regret, make plans to continue the date at another place and time, and take your leave.

You should not invite guests back to your abode if you have experi-enced even the subtlest tremor deep within your bowels. For once an invi-tation for a visit has been extended and accepted, it is rude in the extreme to then suddenly and unexpectedly rescind it. In that situation, when the boiling rumbles are suddenly upon you, you are faced with two evils of equal value: ejecting your guest without explanation, or fumigat-ing them out. Best to avoid both by playing it safe.

Should the turtle not rear its ugly head until you have arrived at your *date's* home for the first (or even second or third) time, then immedi-ately assess your surroundings. If you are certain your deposit will per-meate the walls—either aromatically or audibly—so that your partner is certain to be apprised of your digestive process, then it is wise to remove yourself from the premises for your evacuation and postpone your inter-lude for another time. Remember, do not impose more intimacy on a brand-new relationship than it can handle. After all, a little mystery is what makes those first few dates so magical. Do not spoil it by soiling the toilet with skid marks.

If the situation is not *dire*, and you are quite confident you can handle the situation quickly and quietly, then there are several ways to make the best of a shit situation outlined on the chart on p. 192. Of course, any of these techniques may easily backfire, for each solution may create a new problem. And if your date be particularly clever and observant, you will be given away completely. Therefore, be as discreet as possible. (See chart on p. 192.)

Let us assume you have successfully lightened your load, and returned to the amorous affections of your date, who fortuitously seems blissfully ignorant of your recent activities. If it is agreed upon or blatantly obvious that you will be having your body cavities intimately explored or even if you are simply spending the night, it is completely acceptable—nay, encouraged—to ask your guest if you may take a shower. Explain that it has been a long day and you are feeling grimy, that you always take a shower before bed to relax and keep your sheets clean, or that it is simply a presex ritual for you. Do not—repeat, do *not*—mention that you relieved yourself of some dead weight only minutes earlier. If, for whatever reason, a shower is not possible, then you must find a way to quickly and discreetly rinse your entire crotch in the bathroom, making sure no bits of toilet paper remain behind.

Even if neither of you feels like you have to go, there is always the chance of espying a little dirt should you indulge in anal sex. Mature ladies and gentlemen know this is simply a fact of life. They do not freak out if their ring-finger nail requires a good scrubbing after it has engaged in some poking, nor do they have hissies if the condom does not emerge the exact same color it went in. Of course, this can be avoided for the most part by taking fiber, as previously recommended, and by familiarizing yourself with the correct and polite way to have anal sex.

Menstrual Blood and Other Fun Fluids

A mistake made by many ladies and gentlemen is to assume that sex is not permissible during menstruation (save certain religious traditions).

TECHNIQUE	PROS	CONS
Carry matches on you at all times.	It is not indelicate for one to have matches on one's person (especially if one is a smoker), and it is certainly more convenient and discreet than carrying about an aerosol can. Lighting a match and extinguishing it immediately undercuts any noxious (and obnoxious) smells.	Instead of your poo, your date may smell the match, which is just as much a dead giveaway (albeit a more pleasant one).
Turn on the faucet while you go.	This *should* create enough ambient noise to muffle the piglike squeals emanating from your behind.	If you are not quick about your business, you may give the impression that you are an obsessive-compulsive hand washer. You may even inadvertently offend your date, if he or she be sensitive to environmental issues and water conservation.
Cough.	If your timing is impeccable, you can mask any sounds due to gas or the dreaded "kerplunk."	Your date may fear that you are a secret smoker, or that you have consumption.
Muffle your toots with toilet paper.	If audible gas is your main concern, you can gently press a wad of toilet paper against your anus to muffle the sound.	While this works miraculously well, it must be assumed that blocking the natural passage of gas cannot be great for one's constitution.
Flush twice.	Immediately flushing the toilet as soon as the offending log has been deposited may help whisk away some of the residual odor.	This means you will have to flush again once you have completed wiping, which may suggest to your date that your creation was so massive that it required two flushes to get it down—not a preferable image to evoke before sex.

TECHNIQUE	PROS	CONS
Put liquid soap in the bowl.	If they have liquid hand soap by the sink, a squirt or two before you flush may help freshen the bowl.	Too much may result in an overabundance of suds—a puzzling development for your date to discover when they next use the washroom. You could flush again and again, but then you run the risk of the previous "con."
Pad the bowl with paper.	If your deposit has a particularly large distance to travel before breaking the surface of the water and will therefore likely create a loud noise and an unhygienic splash, you may create a landing pad of toilet paper to break the fall.	This is highly ill-advised, as excessive toilet paper may result in an overflow. Considering the race for a plunger, the intense cleanup, and the chance of your date making visual contact with the recent contents of your rectum, this outcome is one thousand times worse than your date simply guessing that you too, like every human being, go poo.

There is nothing indecorous about nature's way—indecorum is found only in people's juvenile and sexist reactions to it. You, of course, are entitled to your preferences, and there is nothing shameful or wrong in preferring your lovemaking without a hint of crimson. However, it is a breach of etiquette to indelicately impose your own philosophy about the matter onto your partner, so as to insult their own personal views or their body. And should the moon pull on your female partner's loins unexpectedly in the middle of coitus, there shall be no displays of disgust or cries of horror. Even if you both agree to navigate the waters of the Red Sea, resist any immature impulses to let an "Eeew" escape your lips once your journey is over and cleanup is underway. This goes for all bodily fluids, whether they be blood, urine, semen, or female ejaculate. If you fear the sheets will be stained, simply put down a dark towel. And do not suggest that protection is not necessary, for pregnancy is still a possibility, and the likelihood of transmitting some STDs is increased with the presence of blood. (For more on semen, female ejaculate, and urine, see p. 114 and p. 127.)

SAFER SEX

Sex has long been an acceptable dinner-table topic. It is chic to talk dirty, and de rigueur to admit to proclivities from spooning to spanking. However, what you will never hear your friends confess to is that they practice unsafe sex. It is just not the done thing.

Yet unsafe sex is very much the done thing—and not just by uneducated teens or drunk college kids. It is done by people who consider themselves ladies and gentlemen. Smart, decent people who give to charities, march in peace rallies, chew with their mouths closed. People who stock their medicine cabinets with the latest latex products. People you are having *relations* with.

We must resist blaming it on peer pressure, though, or on those insufferable young cads who tell their partners that it feels like clapping with gloves on. Rather, it is a *lack* of peer pressure among adults—a simple, mutual decision to ignore the facts. Like a game of chicken, each waits for the other to proffer the prophylactic until it is, shall we say, game time . . . then game on . . . and then, suddenly, game over.

Call it STD ennui, if you like. Perhaps because the basic facts we know by heart have not been buffeted by frighten-the-horses front-page headlines listing new casualties, or because those casualties all seem to live on another continent, we have become numb to the possibilities. And since AIDS seems more like a permanent but treatable condition here in the West, even the king of STDs has lost a bit of sway.

Therefore, while we are busy putting money in envelopes for "condoms to Africa" campaigns, and condemning other governments and pharmaceutical multinationals for failing to provide reasonably priced drugs, we would do well to remember that charity begins at home. The truly wise ladies and gentlemen know that their breed is not immune to unwanted pregnancies or STDs, that urbanity does not protect against infection. And we are talking not merely about HIV, but also herpes, HPV, gonorrhea, chlamydia, hepatitis B—the list goes on. Prudence dictates that we remain ever diligent about protecting ourselves and our partners. For if etiquette is ultimately designed to keep us from destroying each other, then getting tested regularly, being communicative about our sexual histories, and using protection and birth control is the pinnacle of decent behavior. The lady or gentlemen who does anything less does not deserve the pleasure of their genitals.

It is not an imposition to request getting tested together for all STDs before bumping uglies with a new partner. Nor is it impolite to insist on utilizing STD protection until six months have passed since sleeping with your last previous (or on the side) partners, all your STD tests have come back negative (at the *end* of this period), and your partner has earned your trust.

Condoms

It is every sexually active citizen's duty to come prepared, as it were. Supply yourself with only the best barrier protection: Quality contraception not only reflects well upon your character, it simply feels better. Good ladies, do not expect your male partners to be the sole providers: Do have an opinion on the matter—and supplies on hand. While you can never have too many quality condoms ready for use, you *can* demonstrate too little discretion in their storage and display: An overflowing drawerful by the bed may be misinterpreted by more modest lovers as an indication of your "playa" status. All well-bred lovers familiarize themselves with the proper way to store prophylactics (in a cool, dry, uncramped space out of the sight of neighbors unexpectedly dropping by for a cup of sugar), as well as with the proper use and wear of them (this, dear friends, means reading the instructions carefully).

Even if you have been recently tested, you must honor any lover's request to use protection, for not only is unwanted pregnancy an issue, but there is always the chance you may be a carrier of a disease undetected by the standard battery of tests. It is excessively unbecoming to bemoan the "numbing" ef-

---

Birth Control Etiquette for Gentlemen

Just as it is not automatically the gentleman's responsibility to procure the condom, it is not solely the lady's responsibility to acquire other methods of birth control. Offer to accompany your lady lover to the doctor's office or health clinic. If you are in a committed relationship or even simply having regular sex, it is courteous to offer—insist even—that you share the financial burden of the birth control. If a new birth-control pill gives your girlfriend a case of temporary insanity, always be understanding, compassionate, and patient. Only the savage yields to his baser urges toward exasperated outbursts when his lover happens to be involuntarily riding a man-made, hormone-induced emotional roller coaster in order for you *both* to delight in the benefits of more carefree sex.

---

fects of a condom. And it is outright barbaric to pressure a lover into unsafe sex (or any other sexual practice), especially if said lover happens to be an impressionable and easily swayed young leaf on the tree of sexual experience. And should your condom or dental dam break in the middle of a particularly vigorous session, do not think for even a tick of your pocket watch that "Whatever damage could be done *has* been done, so why bother with protection?" If you are going to continue to play hide the salami, calmly discard the sad vestiges of the broken condom or dam and procure a new one immediately.

Genital Stowaways

We once knew a young man of exceptional character who awoke one day
to a sore upon his regal member. He soon discovered that he, like one in
five Americans, had genital herpes. As a responsible citizen, he vowed to
have the herpes conversation with all his potential partners. During the
first year of his infection, he was valiantly forthright about his disease,
about his feelings for his potential sex partners, and about how they
could be sexually creative with a minimum of risk. However, those conversations always seemed to mark the end of the potential relationship;
the ladies in question invariably phased themselves out of his life after
receiving the news. Alas, overcome by grief, he resigned himself to a life
of abstinence and joined a monastery where he, at present, produces
highly popular compact discs of Gregorian chants.

This sad catastrophe that befell our friend, and many others like him,
could have been avoided. And here we speak not of catching the infection, but rather, of letting the infection ruin one's life. For the disease is
rampant, almost as common as the cold. How you *deal* with a disease
such as herpes is what separates the wheat from the chaff. Our monastic
friend was initially on the correct path. In fact, citizens like him should
receive medals of honor for exhibiting such bravery and honesty in the
face of danger (or, at least, in the face of temporary chastity). If only
everyone felt as compelled as he did to offer up the full scope of their
sexual histories, we would live in a more educated, healthy, and harmonious sexual society. We would be better informed about STDs, and
therefore better equipped to handle such news with aplomb. But instead
of gratitude and praise, his candor was met with rude rejection—a crippling blow from which he could not recover. So please, dear readers, if
you happen to be on the *receiving* end of a conversation like this, enlist
every fiber of your being to receive the news with grace. Honest Abes
should be rewarded for their behavior—not rewarded with unprotected

genital-to-genital contact, of course, but at least with a polite and sympathetic response. Consider that they are probably more informed than most of your less-communicative lovers. Of course, it is every citizen's right to walk away from a partner for whatever reason—but it is unforgivably rude to run. And before turning on our heels to leave, the thoughtful among us will consider for a moment that we could be walking away from our one, true soulmate, and heading toward a future of eternal solitude.

Unfortunately, not everyone is so civilized and considerate, and honesty is not always the quickest route to the most sex. (Hence, so many liars and confidence men . . . who will no doubt find themselves doomed to an eternity of correcting the poor table manners of kindergarteners who have consumed too much chocolate while the hot flames of hell lick their backs.) But if you have been given a gift that may keep on giving, you must confess. Denial, ignorance, horniness, fear of loneliness, or circuitous rationalizations are excuses employed by none but low-bred cretins. Fucking among ladies and gentlemen should not be considered a right, but a privilege—one you must earn through honest communication about your body and where it has been.

Rest assured, the conversation need not be as traumatic as informing an eight-year-old her beloved pony has passed on. First, do not make too great a fuss about it, but do not gloss over it either. It is not impolite to assume your new partners know nothing and to provide them with the basics, for despite the fact that this contemporary culture is soaked in sex, most people are still in the Middle Ages when it comes to STD education. It is incorrect to assume that just because you have a particular ailment, you know how it works across the board: Do your homework so you can accurately answer any questions your partners might have. The Centers for Disease Control have been kind enough to offer a National STD hotline (1.800.227.8922) and a website (cdc.gov). They can answer any questions and also direct you to a local STD clinic for anonymous, free (or at least, inexpensive) help. Other polite people can be found at the Planned Parenthood Federation of America (1.800.230.PLAN or plannedparenthood.org) and the American Social Health Association (ashastd.org).

Next, give your partners space to digest the news. Point them in the direction of the resources mentioned above so they can do their own research and come to an informed decision. Remember, do not ever pressure a partner into an answer, do not tell them how they should feel about it, and do not try to sucker them into falling in love with you before you make your confession. However, hoping with every fiber of your being that they fall in love first is permissible.

 You would do well to avoid mentioning the prevalence of your particular STD with too much fervor when first apprising your partner of your situation, lest you come across as protesting too much. ("Oh yeah? You're dumping me 'cause of genital warts? Well, I bet all your exes were infected *and* lying jackholes to boot.") Instead, simply state the facts, as all the most refined and good-looking citizens with STDs are wont to do.

Finally, if you have an STD—whether it is a parasite such as crabs that can be cured in a matter of days, or a virus such as herpes that you will carry for life—it is imperative above all to be good to *yourself*, both physically and emotionally. Speak with your doctor about the correct treatment—even the viruses with no cure are *treatable* with repressive drug therapies. For example, it is possible to lessen the severity and frequency of herpes outbreaks and also speed recovery from sores with medication. Boosting your immune system will additionally help with the recovery or management of *any* STD, so take multivitamins daily and cut out (or at least indulge modestly in) junk food, alcohol, cigarettes, and drugs. If you are saddled with an STD for life, procure a therapist or a support group, for every citizen deserves someone to whom they can vent. You may even wish to seek out a personals site for people in similar situations. Should you fail to meet the love of your life there, at least you will find consolation, empathy, and advice regarding the big talk. (For a complete guide to all the monsters lurking in the bedroom, check out *The Big Bang: Nerve's Guide to the New Sexual Universe* or simply log on to one of the websites recommended above.)

PERFORMANCE ANXIETIES

We know a lady of good standing who thought she had found the man of her dreams: handsome, charming, intelligent, miraculously modest, well-off, and, most felicitously, well-endowed. The evening had come when they would seal their relationship with a full-body kiss. She quivered with anticipation and expected nothing less than sheer bliss. And so, dear readers, imagine her horror when his tongue attacked her as a leaping lizard's would a fly. The situation worsened when she discovered he was similarly inept in every other way of love: no moves, no subtlety, no tact.

Many an ungratified, flummoxed lover has bitten their tongue and not expressed their frustrations because they were too cowardly to speak up. They either loved the person *once* and left, or they simply settled. No doubt, they believed they were being polite in sparing their lover's feelings, but actually they were shirking their civic duty to impart sexual wisdom to their bedmates. Citizens of the world, it is your responsibility to leave a lover better than you found him or her. Only *you* can prevent abominable sex.

Of course, no one thinks they leave anything to be desired in bed. There may be some who are insecure about their oral abilities or the number of positions and orifices in their repertoire, but *everyone* thinks they have a firm grip on the basics. Everyone believes they are a good kisser. With amorous activities that are considered an *acquired* skill rather than an innate one, giving and getting instruction is expected—encouraged,

even. However, to criticize someone's basic sexual *style*? That is
not unlike telling them they laugh
"incorrectly."

Unfortunately, that is exactly
what the decent among us must
do (in the nicest possible way, of
course) if we wish to undo years of
bad bed habits in a lover—or at least
teach that lover how *we* like our sex.
First, though, we must be certain
that we are not merely mistaking
sexual fascism for sexual education.
We are all individuals and thus have

Apology Not Accepted

Gentlemen and ladies apologize when they accidentally
bump into someone on the
promenade or when they mistake a stranger for someone
they once slept with—*not*
when they fail to come, when
they gag while deep-throating, when
they accidentally queef or toot, or when
they wish to discontinue a particular sexual
activity. One should apologize during sex
only after clonking a lover in the nose with
one's elbow during a 69 or a threeway.

individual tastes. The thoroughbred citizen knows to distinguish between
a lover with all the wrong moves and a lover who simply performs the
moves in a unique order.

Once you have examined your motivations and determined they are indeed philanthropic, you may venture forth with a clear conscience. First,
create an uplifting environment by telling your ingenue all the things you
adore about them, from their modesty to their manhood or maidenhood.
Then you may tell them that you do not quite feel the same connection
when it comes to the carnal, but that you would like nothing more than to
work on generating such a spark. It would be a breech of tact to accuse
them of being a lousy lay; instead, take inspiration from the television
pop psychologists of the world and employ "I" language. As in, "I really
need X, I really like it when you do Y, I was hoping you could ever so gently
stick your Z in my O," rather than, "You're doing it all wrong." In addition,
it is elegant to speak in specifics and positives, that is, "Oh my God, when
you were swirling your tongue in a figure eight over and over it was wicked
awesome," rather than, "For the most part, you suck at going down on
me." But if something is *very* wrong, do not be a martyr and say nothing;

offer kinder, gentler criticism along with practical suggestions. That is: "Just a bit softer, my loveling. Let us fetch some more lube."

Do not attempt to reprogram your partner in one sitting. Vulgarians rush; mature ladies and gentlemen work on such delicate issues in installments. Play little games that save the sex but spare the ego. One night, focus on activities that provide lots of skin-to-skin contact without requiring sex—perchance a full-body massage. This provides an opportunity to enjoy your partner physically without fretting that they will ruin it once the intercourse commences—and it gives them a lesson in sensual finesse. On another night, perhaps announce that you would like to play "Do As I Do": You kiss or touch them in the manner you wish to be kissed or touched, and they follow suit. You must be sure to offer positive reinforcement when they mimic you as precisely as a looking glass. You might also suggest masturbating in front of each other so your student can watch and take diligent notes. More daring ladies and gentlemen might tie up a partner so

Kiss Off

Herein you will find polite excuses that may be employed to help keep a lover's wild tongue in its cage and your relationship on track:

➤➤ **The Public Nuisance:** "Woah there, Nellie, we don't want to frighten the horses. I'm all for PDA, but please let's keep it G-rated for the kids' sake."

➤➤ **The Bored Game:** "I know this really cool game. You have to kiss each other without touching anything except lips, and that includes tongue and all other body parts. Wanna play?"

➤➤ **Foreplay for Fools:** "Honey, I just want you to lie back, relax, and let me do *all* the work. You don't have to move an inch. No, I mean it, don't move!"

➤➤ **The Doctor's Note:** "My dentist said that due to my root canal, no foreign objects may enter my mouth, except through a straw."

➤➤ **The Barry White:** "Aaaaw yeah baby, I just love your beautiful supple lips, oooooh, they're so round and red, oh oh oh, I wanna love them all night long, reeeeeal soft and reeeeeal slow, baby."

➤➤ **The Blunt Instrument:** "I enjoy the wet one every now and again, but people are starting to wonder about the teeth marks. Please be gentle with me from time to time. Now kiss me, you fool!"

they cannot move, carefully place a gag in their mouth so they cannot kiss, and then have their wicked way with them.

Throughout these lessons, it is not impolite to turn dirty talk into instruction—and vice versa. However, you would do well to remember that this is not your own personal vagina monologue: Have your lover tell you what he or she desires and needs, too, lest you come across as a turn-me-on tyrant.

Old Dogs and New Tricks

It is an undeniable breach of etiquette to put so much importance

Impositions

If your partner is attempting a new technique that is leaving you cold, it is incorrect to yawn, breathe a sigh of annoyance, or begin absentmindedly examining your cuticles in order to silently convey a "cease fire." Simply suggest an alternative with a smile or a sultry voice: "Let's try this!" A gentleman or lady avoids demoralizing outbursts such as "No, not there, neophyte!" The occasional "ouch" may be employed in emergencies only, though a gentleman or lady always attempts to smooth over the outburst with a polite laugh after the pain has subsided, so the pleasurer suffers not a severe blow in confidence.

on one particular sex act that, having been denied it, you are willing to give up on an otherwise wholly satisfying relationship. (It is especially odious if that relationship is a marriage.) Threats of abandonment if certain "needs" are not met—like, say, a butt plug up one's arse—are *terribly* tacky. Relationships are about compromise, and sometimes one must give up the gimp outfit in order to gain a lifetime of support and companionship.

Having said that, we would be remiss in our duties if we failed to note that compromise works both ways. Is it not similarly stubborn and ungracious to deny fulfilling a loving partner's particular fancy, simply because of an irrational prejudice formed a lifetime ago? Now, in no uncertain terms are we advocating doing anything you find morally reprehensible, humiliating, or painful—such as watching kiddie porn, wearing a Nixon mask during sex, or taking it up the bum without lubrication—just because someone else requested it. However, we do not see the harm in *safely* dabbling in less traditional sex acts, such as strap-on sex or fisting, with the person you are supposed to share the most intimacy with. Rather than indulging an impulsive, knee-jerk reaction to unfamiliar territories, why not conduct a little research on the topic in question and find out how to make it safe, clean, and enjoyable? If and when you discover your partner's particular penchant *can* be all those things, maybe you will learn to enjoy it, too, like that lovable little rascal Mikey did Life cereal. For there are more sexually fulfilling acts between heaven and earth than are dreamt of in your philosophy.

There is no need to cave completely and become an overnight fisting aficionado or butt pirate of Penzance—it is perfectly polite to indulge certain requests only on birthdays and public holidays. For all those non-special days, it is necessary simply to keep your mind, heart, and body open to new things (within reason). After all, nothing chimes the death knell for a sexual relationship quite like a persistent unwillingness to join a partner on his or her lusty journey.

Terribly Touchy Topics

As Portia argued to the Venetian court, "The quality of mercy is not strained, it dropeth like a gentle rain upon the place beneath." And so should your mercy dropeth upon a lover who suffers from a problem less of style than of equipment.

While women do have their set of physical concerns, it cannot be denied that men bear the brunt of technical difficulties when it comes to performance issues. Well nigh every gentleman has suffered the two most common indignities: failing to stand at attention and arriving unfashionably early. These are especially common (and mortifying) during the dawn of a relationship (when nerves can impede performance), after a long night of drinking, or after a long dry spell. Additionally, some gentlemen

will suffer the opposite indignity (forsooth, it can be an indignity) of arriving unfashionably late—or not at all. Should you be an innocent by-
stander to any of these mechanical failures, do not be so quick to indulge
in trite reassurances such as "It's okay, it happens to everyone," lest you
come across as condescending and insincere. Still less should either of
you make much ado about nothing—it would be melodramatic to self-
diagnose a medical problem based on a single, isolated malfunction.
Rather, refined ladies and gentlemen work around the situation—not ig-
noring the flagging little fellow, and certainly not badgering him into participation, but simply choosing activities he can enjoy at half-mast. The
well-bred gentleman never assumes that an uncooperative member
means the end of the session, but instead treats it as a serendipitous occasion to make his partner the center of attention. His partner accepts
this attention with grace, and does not take personal offense at the lack
of attention being paid on the lower deck. Finally, while the gentleman
may make light of the poor showing with comments such as, "Come on,
buddy, don't let me down here," it is vulgar and mood-destroying to refer
to the sad state of affairs as "beer dick," "droopy dick," "limp dick," or
any other uncouth locution bandied about by the classless masses.

As far as ladies are concerned, there are several misconceptions con-
cerning the sensory indicators that a woman is "into it" that may cause
her or her partner undue stress or concern. For example: If she is wet she
is into it, if she is not she is not—or so the story goes. Natural lubrication
actually happens quite frequently, whether she is in bed or at the grocery
store. However, once in the heat of the moment, automatic production
of love nectar is finite, at least for most women. So during any session
of Olympic proportions, though her head may be in the game, her fluid-
producing glands may be on the sidelines. As Shakespeare so wisely
observed, desire can strangely outlive performance. In addition, lying
horizontally may make it more difficult for the rains to pour down. For
these reasons, it is not impolite to suggest or insist upon the use of
man-made lubrication for any vaginal probing. Pronouncements or

protestations such as "lube is a crutch" are vulgar in the extreme.

Similarly, erect nipples do not always indicate a sexually aroused state. That is a myth propagated by nine-year-old boys who joke about high beams to mask their absolute awe of their (most likely chilly) female peers. Once embraced, it is a myth that is hard to renounce, especially now that teats standing at attention have become a veritable "sexy" fashion accessory (some music and movie stars known for their excessive and garish displays of wealth reportedly employ professional nipple tweakers on their sets). However, an inordinate percentage of women's nipples do not sit up and beg, as it were, when they are, shall we say, *begging* for it. Therefore, do not be disheartened, and certainly do not engage in anything akin to foot stamping should her teats fail to grow like sea monkeys.

Another misguided obsession is the elusive female orgasm. If a woman cannot achieve one through penetrative sex, it is frequently assumed

Say My Name

Should you be thinking of one person whilst you are doing another, avoid verbosity lest you mistakenly call out the wrong name. If you inadvertently speak before you think, remain calm, carry on, pretend you did not even notice the misnomer, and pray to the gods above that your partner did not hear it. If the gods are frowning upon you and your partner *did* hear a third missing party's name, play dumb, but only if you can deliver a convincing performance. Either way, you must ultimately bend to your partner's will with the utmost humility, explain it was simply a matter of misfiring synapses and a slip of the tongue, all the while figuratively (or literally, if they like) bestowing kisses to their posterior. Should you be the recipient of such a dagger to the ear, it is perfectly correct to express outrage and hurt. And it is not impolite to put an immediate halt to the rutting. However, retain some perspective on the matter. Such a situation is not as dire as if your lover actually cheated on you with this third party, though it is of course more disturbing than if your lover had merely shared a platonic cup of coffee with said party. Behave accordingly.

something is broken—whether because of an emotional block (perchance stage fright or father issues) or because of Pavlovian conditioning from her favorite vibrator. These might be legitimate reasons for some women, but for others it is simply the way their bodies operate. Pressure to have goal-oriented intercourse will not help matters any, and is therefore never applied by any respectful and self-respecting citizen. As long as everyone is having a good time, ladies and gentlemen would do well to enjoy the ride, however unorthodox. (For more on orgasm etiquette, see Formal Sex on p. 55.)

There are some uneducated and small-minded louts who would have us believe that salacity, once aroused, allows no room for reason, conscience, or rainchecks. Never before has such poppycock been so widely embraced. It should be enough to merely mention such offensive absurdities in order to condemn them as we ought.

ELEMENTS OF STYLE

Let us imagine that you are in a relationship with someone with whom you are smitten: they are well versed in the ways of amore, wise beyond their years, and possessed of a razor-sharp wit. Most impressively, their table manners are impeccable. And yet, you find yourself in the midst of what might be termed a moral conundrum. Your dilemma? This special someone is severely lacking in one or more of the following departments: looks, hairstyle, fashion sense, endowment, and/or physical fitness. So much so that you cringe whenever you look upon them. Happily, you close your eyes when your lips meet, and your repulsion is temporarily curtailed. You are racked with guilt for abiding by such superficial standards, but you cannot deny your feelings. You tell yourself your intentions are honorable, that you wish to protect them from the judgments of others, but you ultimately fear that *you* will be judged by who you are with. You ask yourself, How can I be so physically attracted to someone who is so aesthetically displeasing to me? In moments of superiority, you tell yourself you are out of your lover's league. And yet, you are in love . . . almost.

If we look to etiquette for insight, we will learn that it is permissible not to be attracted to someone aesthetically speaking, but it is not permissible to be ashamed of them. It is permissible for *you* not to find someone good-looking, but it is not permissible to be so concerned with what others think. It is permissible to think you are out of a person's league in one department; it is not permissible to assume that means you are out of their league in general. It is permissible to judge someone's appearance; it is not permissible to judge someone's *worth* by their appearance. It is permissible to enjoy the hot sex (and the company) without wanting a serious relationship; it is not permissible to let someone *think* you want a serious relationship just to keep the good head and great jokes flowing.

The wise lady or gentleman knows there are myriad factors at play when it comes to sexual compatibility. 'Tis not simply about one single aesthetic concern, 'tis also about chemistry, pheromones, politics, kissing styles, creativity, emotional sensitivity, intelligence, sense of humor, birth-control preferences, kink factor, bedsheet thread count, STD tests, self-esteem, stamina, exhibitionism, ambition, and asparagus intake. To let one superficial factor overrule all others is akin to retiring your worn billfold full of crisp Benjamins to the waste basket simply because the billfold's seam is beginning to fray.

While it is perfectly acceptable to have certain beauty preferences, it is abhorrent to become a beauty fascist. You can neither escape nor deny the facts that with age comes droop, with the blues comes lethargy, and with stress, gray hairs. To be sure, we may *bend* the laws of nature to our vain whims with the help of drugs or surgery, but we cannot break them. We would do well to remember that while looks will certainly fade, personal integrity is forever.

Physical Fitness

Just as smokers should woo fellow smokers, so gym rats should pursue their own kind. For if something so integral to one's persona (as a nicotine or exercise addiction) clashes with a partner's philosophy and habits, the limits of love will be strained on a regular basis—more often than they would otherwise. While people certainly can and do change their ways, it would be a mistake to wed someone simply for their *potential*. It is safer to assume the couch potato will be more prone to abusing the comfort, intimacy, and stability of a relationship, and thus begin to let him or herself go—or go further. Should this assumption prove untrue, what serendipity. If not, at least disappointment will never be an issue.

If you find your once active and vivacious partner suddenly developing a second chin—not as a result of the natural aging process (which you *must* forgive and permit), but as a result of too much brie and baguettes—best to nip it in the bud, for bad habits form quickly and die slowly. Resist the urge to deliver any ultimatums; such gauche threats are beneath you. Instead, offer honest communication in the guise of mutual self-improvement. Count the ways you love and care for your partner, but admit that it pains you to see them not care for *themselves*. Suggest the two of you get in shape together with a regular game of tennis or some Bikram yoga so that you may indulge in acrobatic sex that would make the members of Cirque du Soleil proud. Tell them you would like to start eating more healthily so that when you celebrate your diamond anniversary you will still be able to feed yourselves (or each other, if you like). Ultimately, you must be willing to suffer the same lifestyle changes right alongside your partner, for as with all elements of style, what is good for the goose is good for the gander.

Hairstyles

People are never quite as particular, sensitive, defensive, or inexorable about any other element of style than hair care, especially that of the pubic variety. Many misguided ladies and gentlemen equate being hirsute with being animalistic, and therefore, uncivilized. However, no genetically determined physical trait is inherently gauche—only one's *behavior* is.

How you choose to deal (or not deal) with your own body hair is entirely up to you—that is your right. You may not, however, infringe upon the rights of others by dogmatically presenting your own style as a universal moral imperative, making your case with exaggerated claims about hygiene and impeded oral ability. The *only* body hair that has a trimming law by which all humans should abide is nose hair (see Boogs above)—everything else should be above interrogation or insult.

That said, you can kill unwanted hair with kindness. Never say, "You are going to have to do something with that beaver in your lap if this relationship is to go anywhere," or some such impertinence. Instead, say that you have always wanted to make shaving part of erotic play. Anything you would ask of a partner you must be willing to undergo yourself. If a partner's hair-free asshole is your cup of tea, then be prepared to bend over and spread your own cheeks. You must also be willing to perform the grooming ritual, for if you want something done you must do it yourself—whether that means paying for your partner's procedure or familiarizing yourself with a shaving brush. Please note, though, that nose-hair trimmers or any other hair-removal system do not a romantic gift make.

Once a partner has honored your request, it would be quite horrible of you to criticize the outcome or the stubbly regrowth. The same rules above apply to all upkeep.

Matters of Size

We know a bright young artist who goes by the name of Spencer Tunick. He is renowned in circles far and wide, posh and bohemian, for his group nude shots that are frequently staged, illicitly, in public spaces. Drawing as many as a thousand participants to a shoot, Tunick attracts every walk of life, from the petite college student to the middle-aged pale-ale connoisseur to the wrinkled, revolutionary grandparent. As anyone who has been a subject of his knows, dropping trou', as it were, among hoards of strangers is the antidote to the body-image ennui that plagues so many pop-culture-savvy citizens and porn addicts—that is, those who are ruthlessly bombarded with images of today's "perfect" body. When posing for Tunick, one comes face-to-face with the sights (and smells) of anatomical diversity. One is suddenly struck by the fact that the supermodels of the world are indeed genetic mutants, and the rest of us are merely, beautifully human. Sadly, most polite folk will have neither the opportunity nor the inclination to participate in such a

Clothes and Accessories

A lady never wears condom earrings, panties that shamelessly creep beyond the borders of her clothes, or anything featuring the Playboy bunny icon (even if the intent is ironic). She avoids camel toe at all costs. A gentleman never wears tank tops, sweat pants, earrings, or his mother's underwear. Finally, there is no excuse for either ladies or gentlemen to own, let alone wear, "emergency" underwear. If it is riddled with holes or, heaven forbid, stained, it belongs neither in your intimates drawer nor on your person.

spectacle. And so, as expectations are raised ever higher by modern-day media, insecurity prevails throughout the land.

Considering such a milieu, it would be at the very least indecorous to demand that your partner live up to such ridiculous and impossible expectations, to prey upon their insecurities as if on a fox hunt. Only the malicious and malcontent would complain of a lover's endowment, or press a partner to submit themselves to the knife. Decisions about physical augmentation should be made solely by the individual owner of the body parts in question, and not under pressure from a boorish beau. In fact, as someone's beloved, it is your responsibility to help your partner feel comfortable in their own skin as Mother Nature gave it to them. If penile girth, penile length, cup size, labial size, and/or vaginal elasticity is primary among your priorities, then we highly recommend you abstain from any extended intimate relations with people who fail to meet your standards. It should go without saying that you are never to apprise a prospective partner of their so-called shortcomings.

If you happen to be the red-faced owner of a body part that fails to meet your own self-imposed standards, well, then, you poor, *poor* dear. While we fear the following will fall upon deaf ears, we shall persevere: Please consider for a moment how irrational, self-destructive, and terribly inelegant it is to obsess about your imperfection to point of inhibiting the enjoyment of sex. In all likelihood, you are the only person who finds this offending part so unsexy, while others only notice how unsexy your insecure attitude is. You would do well to either save up for surgery or graciously accept your lot in life as highly desirable, relative to all the sick and starving children the world over.

 Dreams of penile enlargement are best entertained within the confines of one's own imagination, rather than actively pursued in the real world, for your eternal search is sure to yield no more results than those of Sisyphus' labor.

Gentlemen who are plagued with doubts about the size of their specimen have several special considerations. First, take comfort in the fact that, whether extra large or extra small, rarely is the situation as dire as you believe it to be. Next, do not—repeat, do not—mention your "predicament" in a personal ad. We cannot tell you how many men (at least the well-hung ones) make this mistake. This is as uncouth as telling your girlfriend's parents she gives great head, as inappropriate as talking to your dinner guests about the most agreeable bowel movement you experienced that morning, as crass as mentioning your huge schlong in your personal ad. You must also refrain from bringing it up on a date—at least, not seriously. No reaching across the table, touching your companion's hand gently, staring deeply into their eyes and saying solemnly, "There's something you should know about me . . ." or, "I'm not like other guys . . ." Not unless you have no penis, literally. And you should certainly not mention the partners, if any, who have run screaming at the sight of your sausage.

If you unexpectedly discover that he is a she or she is a he, and you feel you have been misled (not unlike Steve Sanders on that classic episode of the television masterpiece, *Beverly Hills 90210*), do not resort to verbal abuse or fisticuffs. Calmly excuse yourself from the awkward situation with a curt, "I feel I have been grossly misled. Good day, sir, er, madam!"

Why, you ask? First of all, a warning will never work the way you wish it to—it will either appall your date or pique their curiosity. But even if they are disgusted, they will probably stick around long enough to satisfy their curiosity (and have a good story to tell their friends). And if their curiosity does not trump their knee-jerk and therefore rude assumptions and reactions, you might have just scared away the one person that would have fit you like a glass slipper. Giving potential suitors a heads-up (or should we say, a heads-down) suggests some kind of medical problem. And mentioning all the size-ists in your past is just bad manners—one should never be forced to imagine the countless other persons one's date has bedded.

The only situation in which it might be acceptable to mention the magnitude of your manhood is if your magnitude is in fact of equestrian proportions and the conversation takes a turn for the saucy. Imagine, if you will, the following scenario: You are out, things are going well, you have partaken of a few cocktails, the innuendoes are flowing freely, your date recounts a suggestive story about that one time at band camp, and you retort with a lighthearted and most humble "I definitely don't mean to toot my own horn, but, well, I happen to have what you might call a, um, tuba in my trousers." Wink wink, nudge nudge. If your date inquires further, you may talk about it very humbly and very vaguely, without going into any gory details. If they do not probe, figuratively speaking, just laugh it off and consider them "warned."

In Conclusion

As with all issues of etiquette, you can only be responsible for yourself. Civility is best propagated by example. Thus, the lady or gentleman who wishes to walk among elegant, courteous, and comely persons would do well to always strive to be elegant, courteous, and comely. It begins with you, dear friend, and if fortune smiles upon you—forsooth, she favors good manners—then it might just end with a similarly thoroughbred citizen in the bedchamber.